The KGB and the Vatican

The KGB and the Vatican
Secrets of the Mitrokhin Files

Sean Brennan

The Catholic Education Press
Washington, DC

Copyright © 2022
The Catholic University of America Press
All rights reserved

Library of Congress Cataloging-in-Publication Data
Names: Mitrokhin, Vasili, 1922-2004, author. | Brennan, Sean (Sean Philip), 1979- editor, translator.
Title: The KGB and the Vatican : secrets of the Mitrokhin files / Sean Brennan [editor and translator].
Description: Washington, DC : The Catholic Education Press, [2022] | Includes bibliographical references and index.
Identifiers: LCCN 2022022349 (print) | LCCN 2022022350 (ebook) | ISBN 9781949822229 (paperback) | ISBN 9781949822236 (ebook)
Subjects: LCSH: Catholic Church--Foreign relations--Soviet Union. | Soviet Union. Komitet gosudarstvennoĭ bezopasnosti--History. | Intelligence service--Soviet Union--History. | Cold War. | Catholic Church and world politics. | Communism and religion. | Soviet Union--Foreign relations--Catholic Church. | Vatican City--Foreign relations--Soviet Union. | Soviet Union--Foreign relations--Vatican City. | Soviet Union--Foreign relations,--1945-1991.
Classification: LCC BX1558.3 .M58 2022 (print) | LCC BX1558.3 (ebook) | DDC 282/47--dc23/eng/20220711
LC record available at https://lccn.loc.gov/2022022349
LC ebook record available at https://lccn.loc.gov/2022022350

"I will be loyal to Soviet authority only when all Communists are religious believers!"

—*Bishop Starkus of the Lithuanian Soviet Socialist Republic*

*Dedicated to all religious believers who lived under
Soviet rule, who kept the flame of faith alight
during seven decades of oppression*

Table of Contents

Introduction 1

The KGB Against the Vatican, by Vasili Mitrokhin 33

Suggestions for Further Reading 99

Index 101

Introduction

One of the greatest ironies of the history of Soviet rule is that, for an officially atheistic state, those in the political police and in the Politburo devoted an enormous amount of time and attention to the question of religion. The Soviet government's policies toward religious institutions in the USSR, and toward religious institutions in the non-Communist world, reflected this. Of these, none dominated the attention of the Kremlin more than the Catholic Church and the state that directed it—the Holy See. The ideological animosity between Catholicism, in both its Roman and Byzantine forms, and Marxism-Leninism stretched back into the nineteenth century. Following the Bolshevik seizure of power in October 1917, the Soviet government considered the Vatican one of its principal ideological and diplomatic enemies—a stance that hardened in the period following the emergence of the Cold War and the outspokenly anti-communist papacy of Pius XII (r. 1939–1958). There were exceptions: Pius' successors John XXIII (r. 1958–1963) and Paul VI (r. 1963–1978) both attempted to open limited forms of dialogue with Soviet satellite regimes in Eastern Europe and, to a lesser extent, with the Soviet government itself. This approach was later named *Ostpolitik* ("Eastern Politics"), after the German term used for Chancellor Willy Brandt's attempt to improve dialogue between East and West in the same time period of the Cold War. The early papacy of John Paul II (r. 1978–2004) coincided with a renewal of East-West tensions and, with it, an end to the Vatican's *Ostpolitik* until the late 1980s and early 1990s, when both the Cold War and the Soviet Union itself were ending.

It is one thing to discuss generalities regarding the hostilities between an atheistic, totalitarian superpower and an ancient religious body with the loyalty of over one billion believers, but primary sources provide a better picture of how this rivalry played out. Documents from the Soviet side, particularly from the main agency of the government assigned to deal with both foreign and domestic enemies—the Committee for State Security (*Komitet Gosudarstvennyoi Besopastnost*, which the West knows as the

KGB)—remain scarce.[1] Fortunately, the KGB archivist and defector Vasili Nikitivich Mitrokhin created voluminous transcriptions and summaries of KGB records that span almost 20 years. These transcriptions contain, among other details, a limited but fascinating account of KGB activities directed against the Holy See from the early 1960s to the early 1980s—the vast majority of which took place during a period when the Vatican was attempting to reach out to governments on the eastern side of the Iron Curtain.

This introduction to the English translation of sections of the Mitrokhin Archive is divided into three parts. The first is an introduction to Vasili Mitrokhin himself and describes the circumstances surrounding the creation of his archive of KGB transcriptions and its eventual transportation to the United Kingdom. The second part discusses the historical background of the relationship between the Soviet regime and the Vatican, leading up to and including the period discussed in Mitrokhin's record. Finally, the third section briefly summarizes the Mitrokhin Archive's revelations regarding the KGB's efforts against the Vatican, both independently and in coordination with political police forces in the satellite regimes in Eastern Europe.

VASILI MITROKHIN AND HIS SECRET ARCHIVE ON KGB'S OPERATIONS

Vasili Nikitivich Mitrokhin was born March 3, 1922 in the village of Yurasevo in the Ryazan Oblast, situated southeast of Moscow, in the Russian Soviet Federative Socialist Republic (RSFSR). He passed away in London on January 23, 2004 of pneumonia.[2] Mitrokhin received his university education in the Kazakh Soviet Socialist Republic, attending the

---

1. The first name of the Soviet political police was the Cheka, a rendering of the Russian acronym for the Extraordinary Committee to Prevent Counter-Revolution and Sabotage. The political police were called by many names during the years of Bolshevik rule over Russia, from the GPU (*Gosudarstvennoye Politicheskoye Upravlenie*—State Political Directorate) to the NKVD (*Narodnyi Komissariat Vnutrennikh Del*—People's Commissariat for Internal Affairs). For simplicity—and following the example of scholars of Soviet intelligence such as Christopher Andrew, Harvey Klehr, and John Earl Haynes—I use the term KGB throughout this introduction.

2. Obituary of Vasili Mitrokhin, *Washington Post*, February 3, 2004, LexisNexis Academic. The title of this obituary succinctly expressed the man's contribution: "Vasili Mitrokhin, 81; Copied KGB Spy Files."

Kharkov Higher Juridical Institute, which had been evacuated from the eastern part of the Ukrainian Soviet Socialist Republic shortly after the German invasion in June 1941.[3] Toward the end of the Second World War, he joined the Military Procurator's Office in Kharkov following that city's liberation from German occupation by the Red Army in August 1943. Four years later, in 1948, Mitrokhin joined the KGB (then referred to as the MGB), headquartered in the enormous former headquarters of the All-Russian Insurance Company at Lubyanka Square in the heart of Moscow. He spent the next decade working for its First Chief Directorate (*Pervoyue Glavnoye Upravlenniye*, PGU), which oversaw all foreign intelligence activities. His work included accompanying the Soviet Olympic delegation to the 1956 Summer Games in Sydney, Australia. This demonstrated a high degree of trust that the KGB had in Mitrokhin, as this was the same year the Communist world was shaken to its core by uprisings in both Poland and Hungary. The beginning of his career in intelligence work for the Soviet secret police was during the late Stalinist period, as KGB operatives were directed to uncover and destroy mostly fictional Titoist and Zionist conspiracies, supposedly engineered by the American CIA (Central Intelligence Agency) and the British MI6 (Military Intelligence, Section 6, also referred to as the Secret Intelligence Service). As a proxy war between the Soviets and the West raged throughout the early 1950s, the threat of a renewal of the Great Terror that characterized the late 1930s was on the mind of every Soviet citizen.[4]

Stalin's death ended the immediate threat of another major purge in the Soviet Union, which, just like the Great Terror of the late 1930s, would

---

3. "Biography of Vasili Mitrokhin," Wilson Center Digital Archive, History and Public Policy Program, Woodrow Wilson International Center for Scholars, 2004. https://digitalarchive.wilsoncenter.org/document/110706.pdf?v=680218c43530a69cb94 11d440a4c5654. Following the German invasion, the Soviet government evacuated hundreds of factories, as well as academic and scientific institutes, from the western parts of the USSR to Central Asia. After the liberation of Kharkov by the Red Army in late 1943, the institute returned to its previous home. Over seventy percent of the city had been destroyed and its population had lost tens of thousands of its inhabitants through starvation, deportations, and executions by the Germans.

4. Christopher Andrew and Vasili Mitrokhin, *The Sword and the Shield: The Mitrokhin Archive and the Secret History of the KGB* (New York: Basic Books, 1999), 1–2.

have targeted the staff of the KGB as well as every other Soviet institution.[5] Three years later, Khrushchev's "Secret Speech" in February 1956 changed the USSR, and the Communist world, forever. Mitrokhin recalled, to his coauthor Christopher Andrew, how he and other KGB agents debated Khrushchev's speech amongst themselves for two days after receiving a letter from the Communist Party's Central Committee that detailed its contents.[6] A combination of factors—including his mild criticisms of certain KGB activities during the Stalinist period and a mistake made on a field assignment—led to Mitrokhin's transfer in 1958 to serve as one of the archive directors of the KGB-PGU, whose records detailed Soviet intelligence efforts abroad.

Unhappy in his new assignment and growing increasingly dissatisfied with the Soviet government, Mitrokhin became an active reader of several Russian writers who were banned under Stalinism, particularly Boris Pasternak, whose poems were widely read in the heady early days of the Thaw. He was outraged by the Soviet Writers' Union's—and, by extension, by Nikita Khrushchev's—criticism of Pasternak's decision to circumvent state

---

5. From 1936 to 1938, the generally accepted time span of Stalin's Great Terror, the Soviet political police—then known as the NKVD—was purged on two occasions. One was when Nikolai Yezhov replaced the NKVD's original director, Genrikh Yagoda, in late 1936; the other was when Yezhov was replaced by Lavrenti Beria in the spring of 1938. Beria served as head of the political police until Stalin's death in March 1953. Considered a likely successor to Stalin, Beria was overthrown by his rival Nikita Khrushchev, who successfully organized the other leaders of the Politburo against him and arrested him during a Politburo meeting in June 1953. Beria was executed, along with a handful of his loyalists, such as Viktor Abakumov and Vsevolod Merkulov, the former head of the WWII Soviet counter-intelligence agency SMERSH (from the Russian phrase *Smert Shpionan* "Death to Spies") in December of that year.

6. Christopher Andrew and Vasili Mitrokhin, *The Sword and the Shield: The Mitrokhin Archive and the Secret History of the KGB*, 3. Khrushchev's "Secret Speech," a five-hour speech given to many foreign Communists as well as the assembled representatives of the Communist Party of the Soviet Union at their Twentieth Party Congress in Moscow in February 1956, criticized numerous aspects of Stalin's rule, particularly his cultivation of a *culti lichnosti* (cult of personality) and his persecution of innocent Communists in the late 1930s and again in the late 1940s and early 1950s. It was the opening salvo of Khrushchev's *ottepel* (the Thaw), a limited attempt to reform the USSR from above—though, as Khrushchev said to his colleagues in the Politburo, "it is being forced on us from below."

censorship by publishing his masterpiece *Doctor Zhivago* abroad in 1958. Even more infuriating for Mitrokhin was the Union's subsequent successful attempt to force Pasternak to decline the Nobel Prize for Literature in Stockholm. Mitrokhin wrote a letter of protest to the newspaper of the Writers' Union, *Literaturnaya Gazeta*; he used his left hand to write, in the hope that his co-workers in the KGB would not recognize his handwriting. His disillusionment grew, however, as Khrushchev's thaw stalled and Khrushchev began acting in the manner of his old boss in suppressing dissent—for example, in Tbilisi and Budapest in 1956 and Novocherkassk in 1962.

Mitrokhin hoped that his own superiors—Chair of the Committee of Party and State Control Aleksandr Nikolaievich Shelepin and KGB Chairman Vladimir Yefimovich Semichastny—would emerge as the new Soviet leaders after they assisted in the peaceful overthrow of Nikita Khrushchev in October 1964. Instead, Khrushchev's protégé Leonid Brezhnev became the new General Secretary of the Communist Party, and Aleksei Kosygin was appointed Head of State. Three years later, Brezhnev removed Shelepin and Semichastny from their posts. This led to the fifteen-year reign of Yuri Andropov as head of the KGB. Andropov soon rose to be the second most powerful person in the Soviet Union. By this point, Brezhnev, Andropov, and other Soviet leaders—such as the foreign minister Andrei Gromyko and ideology boss Mikhail Suslov—ended all aspects of Khrushchev's *ottepel*. They drove the point home by authorizing the invasion of Czechoslovakia in August 1968, to thwart the attempts of the Czechoslovak Communist leader Alexander Dubček to democratize the socialist system.[7]

Because of the renewed repressive atmosphere in the USSR and the information he found examining KGB documents, Mitrokhin gradually began to take steps to oppose the Soviet regime, or at least to document its crimes, by making private copies of its archival records. Although he sympathized with the dissident movement, he did not consider himself a dissident, nor did he consider defecting. From 1974 to 1982, Mitrokhin supervised the moving of the KGB-PGU's archives from Lubyanka to the Moscow suburb of Yasanevo; during this time, he made over 25,000 copies of documents, hiding them under the floorboards of his house. Mitrokhin

---

7. Andrew and Mitrokhin, 5.

retired in 1985. Following the dissolution of the USSR in 1991, Mitrokhin first offered his documents—that came to be known as the Mitrokhin Archive—to the American CIA. When the CIA rejected the documents as possible fakes, Mitrokhin turned to British Intelligence. In March 1992, Mitrokhin brought sample documents to the British embassy in Riga, capital of the newly independent state of Latvia. Following their determination of the authenticity of the documents, MI6 arranged to have him, his family, and his documents expatriated to the United Kingdom.[8] Over the next thirteen years, Mitrokhin wrote three books on the KGB's activities, with MI6's official historian, Christopher Andrew, as coauthor. Mitrokhin served as a regular consultant on the legacy of Soviet espionage before his death in London in 2004.[9] While utilizing the Mitrokhin Archive is not without risk for historians—it contains only Mitrokhin's handwritten transcriptions of KGB documents, with no original documents or even photocopies of them—it remains a valuable resource related to the Soviet secret police's attempts to both enforce Moscow's iron rule within its own borders and extend its influence abroad, as well as revealing the identities of several KGB "illegals," i.e. KGB agents operating under covert identities abroad.[10]

THE KGB VS. THE VATICAN: A HISTORICAL BACKGROUND

The ideological animosity between Marxism-Leninism and Catholicism goes back to at least the mid-nineteenth century. While it is beyond the scope of this introduction to list all the disagreements between the two, it is worth briefly sketching the views of some of the primary philosoph-

---

8. Christopher Andrew, "Vasili Mitrokhin," *The Guardian*, February 3, 2004. https://www.theguardian.com/news/2004/feb/04/guardianobituaries.russia. Mitrokhin would later tell his co-author Christopher Andrew that he considered himself a Russian patriot, and felt the need to document the Soviet regime's crimes as something he owed to the largest group of its victims, the Russian people. According to Andrew, Mitrokhin lived a quiet, private life in Britain, although he did enjoy exploring different parts of the United Kingdom on his rail pass.

9. MI6 stands for Military Intelligence, Section 6. It is also referred to as the Special Intelligence Service, and has directed the United Kingdom's foreign intelligence work since 1909. MI5 is Britain's domestic intelligence service, and the relationship between the two roughly parallels that of the CIA and the FBI in the United States.

10. Andrew and Mitrokhin, 12–17.

ical leaders of each camp. In 1843, in the introduction to his work entitled *A Contribution to the Critique of Hegel's Philosophy of Right*, Karl Marx argued that

> Religion is, indeed, the self-consciousness and self-esteem of man who has either not yet won through to himself or has already lost himself again. Religion is the sigh of the oppressed creature, the heart of a heartless world, and the spirit of a spiritless situation. It is the opium of the people. The abolition of religion as the illusory happiness of the people is the demand for their *real* happiness. To call on them to give up their illusions about their condition is to call on them to give up a condition that requires illusions. The criticism of religion is, therefore, *in embryo, the criticism of that vale of tears* of which religion is the *halo*.
>
> Criticism has plucked the imaginary flowers on the chain not in order that man shall continue to bear that chain without fantasy or consolation, but so that he shall throw off the chain and pluck the living flower. The criticism of religion disillusions man, so that he will think, act, and fashion his reality like a man who has discarded his illusions and regained his senses, so that he will move around himself as his own true Sun. Religion is only the illusory Sun which revolves around man as long as he does not revolve around himself.
>
> It is, therefore, the *task of history*, once the *other-world of truth* has vanished, to establish the *truth of this world*. It is the immediate *task of philosophy*, which is in the service of history, to unmask self-estrangement in its *unholy forms* once the *holy form* of human self-estrangement has been unmasked. Thus, the criticism of Heaven turns into the criticism of Earth, the *criticism of religion* into the *criticism of law*, and the *criticism of theology* into the *criticism of politics*.

Marx further argued, in this work and subsequent writings, that religions had been created by the ruling classes throughout history as a means of social, economic, and political control over the lower classes, by hypnotizing them with dreams of paradise in the next world so that they would be satisfied with their miserable conditions in the world that they actually inhabited.[11] To put it another way, Marx argued "Man makes religion, religion does not make man." Marx proposed the new world

---

11. Andrew McKinnon, "Opium as a Dialectics of Religion: Metaphor, Expression, and Protest," *Critical Sociology* 31, nos. 1 and 2 (2005): 17–18.

that would be born out of his philosophy, grounded in dialectical materialism, a world in which religious beliefs and religious institutions were no longer necessary.[12]

His Russian pupil Vladimir Lenin, a militant atheist like Marx, in his 1909 essay "Materialism and Empiricism," explicitly rejected the idea of his fellow Bolsheviks, Anatoli Lunacharskii and Mikhail Bogdanov, of creating after the revolution a suitable "proletarian religion" without a creator deity.[13] Although considerable scholarship has argued that the ideology of the regime, namely Marxism-Leninism-Stalinism, became a substitute religion for many Communist Party members, this was an attitude sharply rejected by Lenin himself in his pre-revolutionary writings. Lenin emphasized that party members should use their ideological convictions to help believers see through "the religious fog" that had misled them throughout their lives.[14] Following the Russian Revolution and the establishment of the USSR, Lenin continued to articulate these views. In March 1922, shortly before his final physical and mental decline, he published an essay entitled "On the Significance of Militant Materialism," which urged all party cadres to improve their work with the Soviet masses in the dissemination of scientific-materialist propaganda, with the final goal of gradually eradicating religious faith and institutions.[15]

By the time of the October Revolution in Russia in 1917 militant atheism was a central aspect of Communist ideology, with the idea that the future proletarian utopia would be free of religion as a gratefully discarded relic of the pre-revolutionary past. All religious institutions, particularly those with a global reach, were to be regarded as the enemy. As historian Paul Gabel wrote in his work *And God Created Lenin: Marxism vs Religion in Russia 1917–1929*:

---

12. Victoria Smolkin, *A Sacred Space Is Never Empty: A History of Soviet Atheism* (Princeton, NJ: Princeton University Press, 2018), 11.

13. William Husband, *"Godless Communists": Atheism and Society in Soviet Russia, 1917–1932* (DeKalb: Northern Illinois University Press, 2000), 34.

14. Victoria Smolkin, *A Sacred Space Is Never Empty: A History of Soviet Atheism*, 13.

15. William Husband, *"Godless Communists": Atheism and Society in Soviet Russia, 1917–1932*, 59.

Catholicism was resented not only because it blocked the spread of communism, but also because it represented an alternate internationalism already in place. Not only that, it was truly worldwide, while communism lingered at the stage of potentialities. The Catholic Church was a supranational enemy power, and "Christian Universalism" had to be fought. Fearing any rival, the Bolsheviks would have attacked the Catholic Church even if not a single Catholic had lived on Russian soil.[16]

In 1846, the first year of his long papacy, Pius IX—in his first encyclical *Qui Pluribus*—condemned socialism specifically for its atheistic tendencies. He argued that no good Catholic, regardless of whether they follow the Roman or Byzantine Rites, could follow socialist ideals.[17] His more liberal successor, Leo XIII—in his famous 1891 encyclical *Rerum Novarum*—supported labor organizations, social welfare legislation, and a decent wage for industrial laborers. However, he also vigorously condemned socialist ideas. For example, he argued that socialists are "emphatically unjust, for they would rob the lawful possessor, distort the functions of the State, and create utter confusion in the community." Subsequently, after arguing that socialists unjustly attempted to destroy the rightful authority of parents over their children by placing them in the care of a revolutionary state, he condemned its conception of property:

> Hence, it is clear that the main tenet of socialism, community of goods, must be utterly rejected, since it only injures those whom it would seem meant to benefit, is directly contrary to the natural rights of mankind, and would introduce confusion and disorder into the commonweal. The first and most fundamental principle, therefore, if one would undertake to alleviate the condition of the masses, must be the inviolability of private property.

Near the end of the document, Leo XIII memorably referred to socialism as a "fatal plague which insinuates into the very marrow of

---

16. Paul Gabel, *And God Created Lenin: Marxism vs. Religion in Russia, 1917–1929* (Amherst, NY: Prometheus Books, 2005), 374. This argument could apply to the Orthodox Churches as well, although they did not have as great an international reach as the Roman Catholic Church.

17. Peter Kent, *The Lonely Cold War of Pope Pius XII: The Roman Catholic Church and the Division of Europe 1943–1950* (Montreal: McGill-Queen's University Press, 2002), 11.

human society only to bring about its ruin."[18] These condemnations continued up to the late 1930s, given renewed emphasis by revelations of extensive persecution of religious institutions in the USSR, including the closing of the remaining Catholic churches in Moscow and Leningrad. On March 19, 1937, Pope Pius XI released an encyclical, at the height of Stalin's Great Terror, *Divini Redemptoris*, referred to "the 'imminent danger' of Bolshevistic and atheistic Communism, which aimed at upsetting the social order and at undermining the very foundations of Christian civilization."[19]

Following the Russian Revolution and, more specifically, the Soviet-Polish War in 1921, there were approximately 1,200,000 Catholics in the Soviet Union, the vast majority of whom (92 percent) were ethnic Poles. According to a survey of Catholic churches in the Tsarist Empire in 1915, in the territories that would be under Soviet rule from 1921 to 1939, there were approximately 237 Catholic Churches, which were served by 246 priests, including five parishes in Petrograd and two in Moscow.

The Russian Revolution, the Civil War, and the subsequent Soviet-Polish War drastically affected Church attendance—the number of parishioners in Saint Catherine's in Petrograd shrank from 30,000 to 5,000.[20] Most Eastern Rite Catholics of the former Russian Empire, either of Byelorussian or Ukrainian ancestry, dwelt in a region that became part of eastern Poland during the interwar period. There were also a considerable number of Ukrainian Greek Catholics who lived in the territory of Galicia, who had been subjects of the Austrian Habsburgs until 1918 and would spend the next twenty years under Polish rule. Thus, the number of Eastern Rite Cath-

---

18. Leo XIII, *Rerum Novarum: Encyclical on Capital and Labor*, May 15, 1891, http://w2.vatican.va/content/leo-xiii/en/encyclicals/documents/hf_l-xiii_enc_15051891_rerum-novarum. html, PAGE #.
19. Pius XI, *Divini Redemptoris: Encyclical on Atheistic Communism*, March 19, 1937, https://w2.vatican.va/content/pius-xi/en/encyclicals/documents/hf_p-xi_enc_19370319_divini-redemptoris.html, paragraph 3.
20. Gabel, *And God Created Lenin: Marxism vs Religion in Soviet Russia 1917–1929*, 374–377. Saint Petersburg was renamed to the more Russian-sounding Petrograd following the outbreak of the First World War in August 1914; it would be renamed Leningrad ten years later, following the death of Vladimir Lenin. In 1994, it would go back to its old name of Saint Petersburg.

olics in Soviet lands during the interwar era was rather small—when Pope Benedict XV appointed Leonid Fyodorov as head of the Eastern Rite Catholic Church in Soviet Russia, his spiritual jurisdiction covered only twelve parishes with approximately 3,000 members.[21]

The February 1918 Declaration on Church and State by the Bolshevik government, while theoretically not a legal authorization for the persecution of religious institutions in Soviet territories, marked the beginning of seven decades of persecution of all religious institutions in an ultimately failed attempt by the Communist regime to create an atheistic society by force. This did not imply that all religious institutions were persecuted equally, or that the arrests of clergy and the closure of churches followed a predetermined pattern. Patterns of persecution of different religious institutions changed over time. Indeed, the Soviet regime devoted most of its attention to the persecution of the Russian Orthodox Church during the first decade of its rule. However, by the late 1930s, almost all Roman and Byzantine rite Churches had been forcibly closed—the two that remained in operation in Moscow and Leningrad were attended and staffed largely by representatives of foreign embassies. Hundreds of Catholic clergy had joined their Orthodox brethren in Soviet prisons and in the vast network of labor camps, the Gulag.[22]

This persecution continued during the period of the Nazi-Soviet alliance from 1939 to 1941, once the Red Army began conquering the lands guaranteed

---

21. Gabel, 387. The Catholic Church of the Byzantine Rite, also referred to as the Eastern Rite, the Greek Catholic or Ukrainian Greek Catholic Church, was formed in 1595 by the Union of Brest, wherein representatives from the eparchies (dioceses) of the Ruthenian Orthodox Churches in the Polish-Lithuanian Commonwealth agreed to enter into Communion with Rome, as long as they were allowed to maintain their Orthodox liturgical traditions. By the early twentieth century, Greek Catholics could also be found in Carpatho-Ukraine, eastern Slovakia, and northeastern Romania, and in Ukrainian immigrant communities in North and South America.

22. Steven Merritt Miner, *Stalin's Holy War: Religion, Nationalism, and Alliance Politics: 1941–1945* (Chapel Hill, NC: The University of North Carolina Press, 2003), 221–222. *Gulag* was an acronym for *Glavnoe Upravlennie Lagerei* (Main Camp Administration), and was the name given to the vast system of labor camps administered by the Soviet secret police from 1921 to 1987. According to Anne Applebaum's definitive study *Gulag*, over 18,000,000 people were imprisoned in the Soviet labor camp system during its history, and between 4,500,000 and 5,000,000 of those people died during their imprisonment.

to it in the Molotov-Ribbentrop Pact. This included territories with majority Catholic populations, such as Lithuania and western Ukraine. Here, Catholics accounted for 85 percent of the population—approximately 5,500,000 were Roman Catholics, and 3,500,000 belonged to the Byzantine Rite. Once the Red Army arrived in eastern Poland in the fall of 1939 and the Baltics in the spring of 1940, Catholic schools were closed, Church property was confiscated, numerous monasteries and convents were shuttered, and the new Communist authorities initiated a strenuous campaign to promote atheism among the population, especially to children and teenagers. Both the Latin and Byzantine Rite clerical hierarchy were effectively cut off from the Vatican.[23]

The nationalization of religious institutions—including everything from hospitals to orphanages and printing houses—occurred without fail in the territories overrun by the Red Army. In tactics like those used in the Soviet satellite states during the Cold War, theological seminaries were forced to reduce the number of students that they accepted and were eventually closed altogether, including those in the Latvian capital of Riga and in the Lithuanian cities of Vilnius and Kaunas. As the auxiliary bishop of Kaunas, Vincent Brizgys, admitted to the papal nuncio in Berlin in the spring of 1941, it had become effectively impossible for the Church to conduct even the most basic of spiritual activities for its parishioners. During this period, Stalin used methods against the Catholic Church that had pushed the Russian Orthodox Church to the brink of extinction.[24]

The decision by Adolf Hitler to betray his ally Stalin and attack the USSR on June 22, 1941 changed everything regarding Soviet religious policy, at least for the duration of the war. Stalin reached a famous *modus vivendi* with the Russian Orthodox Church, one that would pay dark dividends subsequently, when the Soviet regime assisted the Russian Orthodox Church in absorbing the Ukrainian Greek Catholic Church.[25] The

---

23. Dennis Dunn, "Stalin and the Catholic Church during the Era of World War II," *The Catholic Historical Review* 59, no. 3 (October 1973): 404–408.
24. Dunn, "Stalin and the Catholic Church during the Era of World War II," 410–411.
25. Caroline Dunbar, "World War Two and the Intersection of Soviet Anti-Religious and Foreign Policies in Soviet-Vatican Relations East of the Curzon Line (1941–46)," *Sources and Methods* (blog), Wilson Center, 2020, https://www.wilsoncenter.

Soviet dictator made a less ambitious effort to reach out to the Roman Catholic Church as well, at least for propaganda purposes. In 1944, once Germany's defeat was a foregone conclusion, the Soviet government attempted to cultivate friendships with a certain number of Roman Catholic clergy although, tellingly, not the Vatican; Stalin's contempt for the Vatican was long evident, expressed in his derisive remark to French Foreign Minister Pierre Laval in Moscow in 1935, when he inquired how many divisions the pope had.[26]

Perhaps the most notable, or certainly the most bizarre, instance of détente was the attempt by Soviet Foreign Minister Vyacheslav Molotov to propose an otherwise obscure Polish-American priest, Stanislaus Orlemanski—belonging to the Catholic church in Springfield, Massachusetts—for a high-ranking position in the postwar Polish government.[27] Orlemanski accepted an invitation to Moscow in April 1944, where he stayed in the bridal suite of Moscow's National Hotel.[28] The priest had two lengthy audiences with Molotov and Stalin to discuss the question of religious freedom in the Soviet Union as well as the Soviet leader's views of the Roman Catholic Church. Holding a press conference in Chicago upon his return to the United States on May 12, 1944, Orlemanski noted that Stalin appeared very open and "democratic," and that the Soviet leader convincingly denied

---

org/blog-post/world-war-two-and-intersection-soviet-anti-religious-and-foreign-policies-soviet-vatican. Stalin described this *modus vivendi* as follows: "The war eliminated the contradictions between the church and the state. The believers abandoned their positions of rebellion, and the Soviet government abandoned its own militant position toward the religion."

26. Winston Churchill, *The Second World War, Volume I: The Gathering Storm* (Boston: Houghton Mifflin Harcourt, 1983), 108. Ironically, Napoleon had made a similar remark about Pope Pius VII: "Am I to treat him as if he has 200,000 men under arms?"

27. Stalin broke relations with the Polish Government-in-Exile in London in the fall of 1943 over the Katyn affair, following the German discovery of the bodies of thousands of Polish army officers executed by the Soviet secret police in April and May 1940. In the spring of 1944, Stalin placed a Committee of Polish Communists in the city of Lublin, the first Polish city liberated by the Red Army. The Lublin Committee, as it was known, soon emerged as an alternate government to the one in London, one that Stalin planned to impose on the entire country after the conclusion of the war.

28. "Foreign News: In Freedom's Name," *Time*, May 15, 1944, http://content.time.com/time/magazine/article/0,9171,850540,00.html

persecuting religious institutions. In addition, Stalin expressed great hope that the Vatican and the Soviet government could become allies in the fight against religious persecution.[29] The main newspaper of the Communist Party of the Soviet Union, *Pravda*, played up the meeting with Orlemanski and Stalin with two front-page articles. The Vatican was not pleased with Orlemanski's actions, however, removing him from duty in Springfield and reassigning him to a monastery.[30] He apologized to his bishop, in writing, and was soon reinstated.[31] It was clear that Stalin had extended the invitation to Orlemanski with an eye toward managing his postwar confrontations with America and the West. A year before Orlemanski's press conference, at a meeting of the Soviet State Defense Committee chaired by Stalin on June 4, 1943, a directive was sent out to all Foreign Intelligence agents abroad that gaining information about and infiltrating religious institutions abroad was now a top priority.[32]

If Stalin was hesitant about renewing his persecution of the Roman Catholic Church in Lithuania or engaging in a propaganda offensive against the Pope during this era, he showed no hesitation regarding the persecution of Byzantine Rite Churches, particularly in Western Ukraine. While the atheistic impulses of Stalinism played a vital role in these policies, the Soviet government also considered the Ukrainian Greek Catholic Church, particularly in Galicia and Volhynia, as a vital contributor to the Ukrainian nationalist sentiment, the destruction of which was vital to the Soviet goal

---

29. "Record of a Conversation between I. V. Stalin and the Roman Catholic Priest Stanislaus Orlemanski about the Feelings of the Polish Nationals in the United States toward the USSR," April 28, 1944, History and Public Policy Program Digital Archive, Vostochnaia Evropa, vol. 1, ed. G.P. Murashko et al., trans. Svetlana Savranskaya, 36–42 (AVPRF, f. 6, op. 6, p. 42, d. 548, 1. 9–15). http://digitalarchive.wilsoncenter.org/document/123130

30. Miner, *Stalin's Holy War*, 166–169. In keeping with obvious PR stunts such as this, the Soviet authorities initially moved cautiously in the immediate postwar period in dealing with some outspoken opponents, such as the Lithuanian Catholic priest and a former leader of the country's Christian Democratic Party, Adam Stankevich.

31. "Suspension of Father S. Orlemanski Lifted by Bishop," *The Observer*, May 21, 1944, http://obs.stparchive.com/Archive/OBS/OBS05211944p01.php

32. Adriano Roccucci, "Moscow and the Vatican's Ostpolitik in the 1960s and 1970s: Dialogue and Antagonism," in *The Vatican "Ostpolitik" 1958–1978: Responsibility and Witness during John XXIII and Paul VI*, ed. András Fejérdy (Rome: Viella, 2015), 64.

of pacifying and absorbing western and central Ukraine in order to incorporate them into the Ukrainian Soviet Socialist Republic after 1945. As historians Andrew Drummond and Jacek Lubecki concluded, "a merger of different strains of Galician political culture manifested as a clandestine practice of the Uniate religion became the glue holding together the most politically aware, nationalistic and religious section of the Ukrainian population concentrated in Galicia."[33]

The hostility of the Soviet government toward the Ukrainian Greek Catholic Church also represented continuity between the Tsarist regime and its successor. This is illustrated by a 1915 quote from Count Vladimir Alekseivich Bobrinskii, the newly appointed Russian governor of former Austrian Habsburg territories in Galicia, to the French ambassador, "I recognize only three religions in Eastern Europe: the Orthodox, the Catholic, and the Jewish. The Uniates are traitors to Orthodoxy, renegades, and apostates. We must bring them back to the true path by force."[34] Given the ferocity of the Soviet persecution of the Ukrainian Greek Catholic Church from 1939 to 1941, numerous Ukrainian Greek Catholics—including the Metropolitan Archbishop of Lviv, Andrei Sheptytsky—hoped that the German invaders in June 1941 would prove to be liberators from Soviet tyranny. Sheptytsky's hopes were quickly dashed, as the Nazis quickly proved that they had come as enslavers, not liberators. He admitted as much in a letter to Pope Pius XII in August 1942, stating, "Today the whole country is agreed that the German regime, perhaps to a greater degree than the Bolshevist one, is evil, indeed even diabolical. For half a year, not a day has passed that the most horrible crimes have not been committed. The Jews are the first victims."[35]

---

33. Andrew Drummond and Jacek Lubecki, "Reconstructing Galicia: Mapping the Cultural and Civic Traditions of the Former Austrian Galicia in Poland and Ukraine," *Europe-Asia Studies* 62, no. 8 (October 2010): 1321. George Kennan, US Diplomat and policy strategist, perceptively argued the Soviet government was eating more than it could digest by re-absorbing the Baltic States and western Ukraine, as these territories were usually the most troublesome for Moscow in the post-WWII era and their drive for independence in the late 1980s and early 1990s would play an instrumental role in the breakup of the Soviet Union.
34. Miner, 14.
35. Miner, 181.

Upon the withdrawal of the Nazi forces and the return of the Red Army to Lviv in July 1944, Sheptytsky released a statement to welcome the return to Soviet authority and calling on the soldiers of the Ukrainian Insurgent Army (*Ukrayinska Povstanska Armiya*, UPA) to lay down their arms. Four months later, in November, Sheptytsky died; he was replaced by Metropolitan Josyf Slipyj as the new Archbishop of Lviv and head of the Ukrainian Greek Catholic Church. Like his predecessor, Slipyj attempted to avoid conflict with the Soviet authorities in the immediate aftermath of war. Fearing a renewal of the persecutions that the Church suffered during the 1930s, he visited Moscow in December 1944 to attempt to reach an accommodation with both the Soviet government and the Russian Orthodox Church.[36]

Slipyj's efforts proved to be for naught, as he and all eleven of the other Ukrainian Greek Catholic bishops were arrested in April 1945; this was followed by the arrest of over 200 other priests. Almost all of them were convicted on charges of collaboration with the German occupiers or with the Ukrainian Insurgent Army and deported to the Gulag. On March 8, 1946, many of the remaining Eastern Rite clergy supposedly signed a public statement asking to reunite with the Russian Orthodox Church and to break away from Rome. The next day, the notorious "Synod of Lviv" took place at Saint George's Cathedral, where the attendants renounced the 1595 Union of Brest—which had created the Catholic Churches of the Eastern Rite—and expressed their intention to re-enter communion with Moscow. This marked the "official" dissolution of the Ukrainian Greek Catholic Church in the Ukrainian SSR; similar methods brought the churches in eastern Slovakia and the Trans-Carpathian region of Romania under the jurisdiction of the Russian Orthodox Church. This was a shameful chapter, not just for the Soviet government but also for the hierarchy of the Russian Orthodox Church in Moscow, which was a willing accomplice.[37]

---

36. Dunn, 422–423. The belief that Sheptytsky's limited public expressions of hope in the summer of 1941 that the Germans would restore religious freedom doomed the Ukrainian Greek Catholic Church in Stalin's eyes is almost certainly overstated. The Soviet government had clear ideological reasons for pursuing their course of action toward the Eastern Rite churches after the war, regardless of what had happened between 1941 and 1944.

37. Kent, 99. The suppression of the Eastern Rite churches was a long-desired goal of both religious and political leadership in Moscow.

The story does not end there. Slipyj spent the next eighteen years in various Soviet labor camps, continually refusing early release in exchange for accepting the decision of the Synod of Lviv and submitting to the authority of the Russian Orthodox Church. Supported by the Vatican and Ukrainian communities abroad, the Ukrainian Greek Catholic Church operated underground for the next forty years, as clergy and laity strove to keep the Church's rituals and beliefs alive. Although the UPA was eventually defeated by the Red Army and the KGB by the early 1950s, Moscow never forgot the role of the Eastern Rite Churches as centers for Ukrainian nationalist sentiment. Over the next four decades, the KGB continually attempted to discover and suppress the activities of those involved in underground Byzantine churches, until Gorbachev relented (and, by extension, on the persecution of other religious institutions) in the late 1980s.[38] As Slipyj said upon his release, "Our priests were given the choice of joining 'the Church of the Regime' and thereby renouncing Catholic unity, or enduring at least ten years of the harsh fate of deportation and all the penalties associated with it. The overwhelming majority of priests chose the way of the Soviet Union's prisons and concentration camps." Only two out of the twelve Ukrainian Greek Catholic bishops survived their prison sentences, and thousands of Eastern Rite believers became martyrs to their faith in the snows of Siberia and Kazakhstan.[39]

Stalin's cruel treatment of the Ukrainian Greek Catholic Church, along with Pius XII's strong anticommunism, made it unlikely that there would be any type of working relationship between Moscow and the Vatican during the remainder of Pius' papacy. The Soviet conquests in the Second World War brought numerous countries that had a Catholic majority either under Soviet influence or under direct Soviet control. Czechoslovakia, Hungary, and Poland were all part of the "Soviet bloc" for the next forty years, while the Baltic States, western Byelorussia, and western Ukraine were directly absorbed into the USSR. In the former territories of eastern Poland—which were made part of the Byelorussian and Ukrainian SSRs—Roman Catholics numbered 4,023,800, or 33.6 percent of the population. Byzantine Catholics, many of whom continued to practice their faith clan-

---

38. Drummond and Lebecki, "Reconstructing Galicia: Mapping the Cultural and Civic Traditions of the Former Austrian Galicia in Poland and Ukraine," 1322.
39. Andrew and Mitrokhin, 498.

destinely after the Synod of Lviv, numbered 3,028,200, or 25.3 percent of the population. While Catholics formed only a tiny minority of the population of Estonia, they comprised 25 percent of the population in Latvia, and in the historically Roman Catholic Lithuania, they constituted 87 percent of the population.[40] Just as in the Ukrainian SSR, the Soviet regime viewed the Catholic church in Lithuania as a center of both religious and nationalist resistance to Communism, a view that lasted for decades. The establishment of field offices of the Institute for Scientific Atheism (*Institut Nauchnogo Ateizma*, or INA*)* in Kiev in 1977 and Vilnius in 1983 demonstrated how seriously Moscow took the threat, as the INA was founded in Moscow in 1964 as the primary Soviet institution to promote atheism over religious belief in the USSR.[41]

Apart from the treatment of Archbishop Slipyj and the Ukrainian Greek Catholic Church, other high-profile prosecutions of leading Catholic clergy—particularly Hungary's Cardinal József Mindszenty and Croatia's Cardinal Alojzije Stepinac—made it unlikely that Pope Pius XII would desire to make any kind of accommodation with Stalin during the early years of the Cold War. Stalin's death in 1953 did not immediately improve matters concerning religious policy, and his successor Nikita Khrushchev was arguably worse than Stalin had been in the post-WWII period, despite Khrushchev's reputation as a political reformer. Little dialogue was possible with a leader who boasted that he would make the last religious believer in the Soviet Union appear on television and force him or her to renounce their beliefs.[42]

---

40. Miner, 222. Communist Yugoslavia had a significant number of Roman Catholics as well, especially in Croatia; however, it was not under Soviet influence in the same manner as Hungary, Czechoslovakia, and Poland. Yugoslavia's independence from Moscow was at the root of the contentious relationship between Stalin and the Yugoslav Communist dictator, Josip Broz Tito. Tito's unwillingness to submit to Moscow's direction led to Stalin's expulsion of Yugoslavia from the Cominform, the international organization of communist parties (https://www.britannica. com/biography/Josip-Broz-Tito).

41. Smolkin, 219. The persistence of religious belief in the USSR, including secretly by some Communist Party members, was a very difficult issue for the INA during the Brezhnev era, coinciding with the general weakening of the hold of the regime's ideology over much of the Soviet population.

42. William Taubman, *Khrushchev: The Man and His Era*, (New York: W.W. Norton and Company, 2003), 513.

The election of Pope John XXIII in 1958, following the death of Pius XII, began a gradual but fundamental reorientation of the Vatican's policy toward the Communist world, one that continued for the next twenty years under both John XXIII and his successor Paul VI. Retroactively referred to as an *Ostpolitik* by historians and political scientists for its resemblance to similar policies pursued by Chancellor Willy Brandt of West Germany a decade later, the Vatican attempted to open lines of communication with various Communist regimes. They were initially more successful in Poland, where the Catholic Church had more freedom of action than anywhere else in the Communist world, and to a lesser extent in Yugoslavia and Czechoslovakia. Relations between Budapest and the Vatican, in particular the question of the appointment of bishops, remained mired in the controversy over the status of Cardinal Mindszenty, an "internal exile" at the American embassy in Budapest since November 1956. Vatican efforts at establishing greater cooperation with Moscow were also limited throughout most of the Khrushchev era. However, there was a breakthrough of sorts in January 1963, where lobbying from both John XXIII and the American President John F. Kennedy convinced Khrushchev finally to release Archbishop Slipyj from imprisonment and allow him to leave the USSR.[43] John XXIII's plea for peace during the era of Mutually Assured Destruction,[44] articulated fully in his famous 1963 encyclical *Pacem in Terris* ("Peace on Earth"), published on April 11, 1963, also attracted considerable attention from the Soviet government, as a number of sections from it were reprinted in the Soviet newspaper *Izvestiia* ("News") later that year.[45]

---

43. John Kramer, "The Vatican's 'Ostpolitik,'" *The Review of Politics* 42, no. 3 (July 1980): 298.

44. Mutually Assured Destruction (MAD) is a "principle of deterrence founded on the notion that a nuclear attack by one superpower would be met with an overwhelming nuclear counterattack such that both the attacker and the defender would be annihilated." First articulated as a doctrine by U.S. Secretary of Defense Robert S. McNamara in 1965, it expressly targeted Soviet cities if the U.S.S.R. attacked the U.S. with nuclear weapons. The belief underlying the doctrine was that the threat of mutual annihilation would serve as an effective deterrent to nuclear conflict. The term "Mutual Assured Destruction" was given to the doctrine by one of its critics, military analyst Donald Brennan. *Encyclopedia Britannica Online*, s.v. "mutual assured destruction," accessed November 24, 2021, https://www.britannica.com/topic/mutual-assured-destruction.

45. Adriano Roccucci, "Moscow and the Vatican's Ostpolitik in the 1960s and 1970s: Dialogue and Antagonism," 71. *Izvestiia* was rivaled only by *Pravda* ("Truth") as

The early 1960s brought a change in leadership to both Moscow and the Vatican, as Paul VI was elected as the new pope in June 1963 following the death of John XXIII, and Leonid Brezhnev became the new General Secretary of the Communist Party of the Soviet Union following his successful *coup d'état* against Khrushchev in October 1964. That same year, Paul VI appointed Archbishop Agostino Casaroli, a strong advocate for normalizing relations with Communist regimes, as the Vatican Secretary of State with a special responsibility for relations with Eastern Europe. After the Cuban Missile Crisis of October 1962 brought the world to the brink of Armageddon, much of the diplomatic leadership of the Vatican felt that some kind of dialogue with the Kremlin and its satellite states was necessary, even if it came at a high cost. Their efforts bore dividends, such as the reestablishment of diplomatic ties with Tito's regime in Yugoslavia and securing the release of both Czechoslovakia's Cardinal Josef Beran in 1965 and Hungary's Cardinal József Mindszenty in 1971. With the authorization of the Soviet regime, a delegation from the Russian Orthodox Church, which included several KGB agents, attended the Second Vatican Council as observers, joining delegations from other Orthodox and Protestant Churches.[46]

Furthermore, in September 1964, following five meetings over the previous sixteen months between Casaroli and the director of the Hungarian Church Office József Prantner in Budapest, the Vatican reached an agreement with János Kádár's government about the appointment of bishops of the Hungarian Catholic Church, which the regime in Budapest would select following consultations with the Papacy. It was the first formal diplomatic agreement between the Vatican and a Communist regime since 1922 and allowed several vacant positions to be filled in dioceses throughout Hungary. This also paved the way for a delegation of Hungarian clerics, including a few undercover agents of the Hungarian secret police, to attend the

---

the most famous and widely read newspaper in the Soviet Union. Much like *Pravda*, the fact the newspaper was full of propaganda from the Soviet Union's Communist Party led to a famous Soviet joke, *Neito Pravda iz Izvestia i iz Izvestia neito Pravda* (There is no truth in "News" and there is no news in "Truth").

46. John Conway, "Vatican Diplomacy Today: The Legacy of Paul VI," *International Journal* 34, no. 3 (Summer 1979): 466–467. Beran had been under house arrest in Prague since 1949, while Mindszenty had been living in exile at the American embassy in Budapest since the Soviet invasion of Hungary in November 1956.

Second Vatican Council. This agreement was reached over the objections of Cardinal Mindszenty.[47] According to a recent study by Hungarian historian András Fejérdy, Kadár's regime was open to dialogue with the Vatican and with some elements of the Catholic Church in Hungary, not only as part of Kadár's broad attempt to reconcile some hostile elements to the regime in the early 1960s, but also to avoid the Church leadership "forming a unitary reactionary bloc" against the regime.[48]

Casaroli summed up the Vatican's *Ostpolitik* by stating that it was "in a certain sense an homage to those who, by their loyalty, made it possible to the church to survive, and who have hereby convinced others to resume a dialogue with it."[49] Outwardly, Casaroli projected the image of a moderate diplomat who was far less hardline in his views on communism than his predecessors were, although his memoirs reveal a clear antipathy to the Soviet government and the various satellite states in Eastern Europe. Nor were the representatives of Communist regimes who negotiated with Casaroli deceived by his benign façade, viewing him as hostile to their ideology. Their beliefs were strengthened after the KGB bugged the Cardinal's offices: According to historian John Koehler, this was done through the connivance of Casaroli's nephew Marco Torretta and his Czech wife, Irene Trollerova (later dubbed "the Vatican Mata Hari" by the Italian Press).[50]

There was also a series of meetings between the Papacy and high-ranking Soviet officials. Soviet premier Nikolai Podgorny met with Paul VI in 1967, while Soviet Foreign Minister Andrei Gromyko met with the pope six times from the late 1960s to the late 1970s—something unthinkable during the days of Communist show trials of high-ranking Catholic

---

47. Hansjakob Stehle, *Eastern Politics of the Vatican 1917–1979*, trans. Sandra Smith (Athens, OH: Ohio University Press, 1981), 314. The earlier agreement, in 1922, was between the Vatican and the Soviet government concerning famine relief in the USSR, especially in areas inhabited by Roman and Byzantine Rite Catholics.
48. András Fejédy, *Pressed by a Double Loyalty: Hungarian Attendance at the Second Vatican Council 1959–1965*, trans. Matthew Caples (Budapest: Central European University Press, 2016), 331.
49. Stehle, *Eastern Politics of the Vatican 1917–1979*, 6.
50. John O. Koehler, *Spies in the Vatican: The Soviet Union's Cold War Against the Catholic Church* (New York: Pegasus Books, 2003), 25. According Koehler, Torretta had been a KGB agent for years before taking part in the bugging operation.

clergy in the late 1940s and early 1950s. According to the memoirs of Y.E. Karlov—a Soviet specialist concerning the Catholic Church who would later become the first official ambassador of the USSR to the Vatican during the Gorbachev era—Paul VI avoided discussing the status of the Catholic Church in the USSR in most of his meetings with Gromyko. The pope was "almost apologetic" when he did bring up requests for even minor concessions from the Soviet regime, although he did conclude a conversion with the Soviet Foreign Minister by saying that the Church could not "remain indifferent" to the position of religious believers in Soviet territories. Nor did these meetings change the fundamental views of Brezhnev, Podgorny, and Gromyko toward the Vatican, which remained hostile and suspicious.[51]

For example, a report to the Central Committee by KGB chief Vladimir Semichastny on January 28, 1966, composed by Sergei G. Bannikov, the head of the KGB's Second Directorate, described the Vatican's *Ostpolitik* as "diversionary maneuver" to distract the attention of the Kremlin from the reactionary activities of "foreign religious centers" in the USSR. Five years later, a 1971 report from the head of the KGB's Fifth Directorate Filipp Bobkov made a similar argument, mentioning how considerations of the Vatican's *Ostpolitik* should have no impact on the Kremlin's awareness that "the Vatican remained one of the most active forces of reaction with a well-organized apparatus, without changing the anticommunist orientation of its ideology and its policy."[52]

These tactics by the Papacy came with considerable criticism from their own side: several Catholic clergy and laity argued that the Vatican's *Ostpolitik* came with a high moral cost but yielded ultimately negligible results. Cardinals Mindszenty and Slipyj were particularly vocal in denouncing the Vatican, with Slipyj making a fiery speech to the Synod of Bishops at the Vatican in 1966, calling for policies that recognized Communist rule as spiritually and politically illegitimate: "Even if the World perish, let justice prevail." Despite this, *Ostpolitik* continued into the 1970s in Lithuania, which

---

51. Nadehzda Belyakova, "The Ostpolitik of Paul VI: Soviet Sources and Research Perspectives," in *The Vatican "Ostpolitik" 1958–1978: Responsibility and Witness during John XXIII and Paul VI*, edited by András Fejérdy (Rome: Viella, 2015), 127–128.

52. Roccucci, 81.

had the USSR's largest population of Roman Catholics, as the Vatican agreed to appoint bishops who would not cause trouble for the regime."[53]

This last policy was definitely in the interest of Moscow, as Lithuania was one of the most troublesome republics in the USSR. In the early 1970s, there was a wave of demonstrations against the Soviet regime, including the self-immolation of several Lithuanian university students in the cities of Vilnius and Kaunas, imitating similar protests in Czechoslovakia during the late 1960s in the aftermath of the Prague Spring.[54] Further, at the end of the decade, another wave of instability broke out in Poland, coinciding with the election of the first Polish pope. Karol Wojtyła, the Bishop of Krakow, became John Paul II, the first non-Italian pope in over five centuries. A protégé of Warsaw's long-serving Cardinal Stefan Wyszyński, John Paul II followed his mentor's approach, prudently selecting his battles with the Communist regime and opposing them when circumstances dictated this was a realistic option. His earliest actions as pope indicated that he would no longer strictly follow the *Ostpolitik* practiced by his predecessors John XXIII and Paul VI: The new pontiff sent his cardinal's zucchetto to the Church of Mercy in Vilnius, which had been a center of religious protest against Soviet rule throughout the 1970s, and also assured the audience during his first official visit to the city of Assisi that he spoke for the "silenced Churches" of Eastern Europe.[55]

Since the imposition of Communist rule over Poland by the Red Army after the Second World War, the regime in Warsaw was mired in chronic instability, greater than that of any other Soviet satellites during the Cold War. The Solidarity Crisis from 1980–1981 was the latest of a long series of periods of political and social unrest in Poland, such as in 1956, 1968, 1970–1971, and 1976. The General Secretary of the Communist-dominated Polish United Worker's Party, (*Polska Zjednoczona Partia Robotnicza,* or *PZPR*,

---

53. Conway, "Vatican Diplomacy Today: The Legacy of Paul VI," 468–469. The Baltic States, particularly Lithuania, were the only parts of the Soviet Union where the Catholic ecclesiastical structure remained largely intact following the imposition of Soviet rule. As the quote from Bishop Starkus at the beginning of the introduction indicates, certain Lithuanian bishops were more obedient than others.
54. David Kowalewski, "Lithuanian Catholic Protest," *The Catholic Historical Review* 67, no. 1 (October 1981): 623.
55. Andrew and Mitrokhin, 511–512.

created by a forced merger of the Polish Socialist Party with the Communists in 1948), followed a pattern that occurred throughout the Soviet bloc during this period. Edvard Gierek had spent much of the previous decade using loans from Western governments to improve the living standards in the country; however, by the late 1970s, there was no more money to borrow, resulting in devaluation of the currency and shortages of consumer goods. His successor from 1980 to 1981, Stanisław Kania, was no more successful in resolving these problems. Thus, the political, economic, and social environment of the country was already set for another uprising on the part of the disgruntled population, and the catalyst for this was a labor dispute in the Gdansk Naval Shipyards in August 1980. Following the firing of veteran crane operator Anna Walentynowicz for engaging in organizing workers without the permission of the PZPR, her colleagues—particularly electrician Lech Wałęsa—rallied around her efforts. On August 17, 1980, they formed a labor organization called *Solidarnosc* (Solidarity), the first labor union independent of the Party's control in the Communist World. Eventually, *Solidarnosc* was seen by millions of Poles as something more than an independent labor union, namely as a government of their own, something that Poland had lacked since 1939.[56]

John Paul II provided crucial moral and spiritual support not just to *Solidarnosc* but to all those who struggled under Communist rule. His pilgrimage to his Polish homeland in June 1979 was a pivotal moment in the history of the Soviet bloc, not only for the millions of believers who attended the religious services he led, but also for his message, which called on Poles to regain their country's destiny and to no longer live in fear. He also expressed repeated support for *Solidarnosc*, including its challenge to the PZPR's stranglehold on Polish political and economic life. Consequently, this made him one of Communism's primary enemies in the eyes of the Soviet leadership—particularly KGB director Yuri Andropov, who had been effectively running the Soviet state as Leonid Brezhnev entered his final

---

56. Magdalena Kubow, "The Solidarity Movement in Poland: Its History and Meaning in Collective Memory," *The Polish Review* 58, no. 2 (2013): 6–11. Under considerable pressure from Moscow, Poland's military dictator General Wojciech Jaruzelski declared martial law in Poland in December 1981, which drove *Solidarnosc* underground; however, it re-surfaced in 1989 to lead the democratic revolution that finally ended Communist rule.

physical and mental decline by the late 1970s.[57] This takes the historical chronology up to the early 1980s, where Mitrokhin's archive concludes with regard to its information on the KGB's policy toward the Vatican.

MITROKHIN'S REVELATIONS ABOUT THE KGB'S VATICAN POLICY: A BRIEF SUMMARY

The Mitrokhin Archive generally supports the traditional analysis that the Soviet government was fixated on "subversive" religious institutions and used its political police, the KGB, to spy on them, infiltrate them, and weaken them. In particular, the activities of the Eastern Rite Churches in the Soviet Union, and their connections to the Vatican, are the focus of numerous KGB reports in the Mitrokhin Archive.

The general Soviet hostility and suspicion toward the Vatican as one of their primary subversive opponents abroad—again, a frequent topic in traditional discussions of Soviet foreign policy—is also a recurring theme throughout the Mitrokhin Archive. Even when the KGB reports the slightly more "progressive" foreign policies of the papacies of John XXIII and Paul VI, the very next paragraph—or even the next sentence—discusses how the Vatican provided financial and ideological support for the Eastern Rite Churches in the USSR and/or the Catholic Church in the satellite states, particularly Czechoslovakia, Hungary, and—of course—Poland. Coordinated efforts between the KGB and the secret police agencies in the satellite states are also mentioned frequently throughout the collection. The use of the archive's material in an article for the online historical journal *War on the Rocks* reinforces this point. Written by Aaron Bateman and titled "Espionage and the Catholic Church from the Cold War to the Present," it discusses how the KGB used its agents placed in the clerical hierarchy of the Lithuanian Catholic Church to infiltrate the Vatican, efforts that were only sporadically successful.[58]

---

57. Gracjan Kraszewski, "Catalyst for Revolution: Pope John Paul II's 1979 Pilgrimage to Poland and Its Effects on Solidarity and the Fall of Communism," *The Polish Review* 57, no. 4 (2012): 29–30.

58. Aaron Bateman, "Espionage and the Catholic Church from the Cold War to the Present," *War on the Rocks*, June 17, 2019, https://warontherocks.com/2019/06/espionage-and-the-catholic-church-from-the-cold-war-to-the-present/. Bateman notes

The documents in the Mitrokhin Archive on Soviet policies towards the Vatican, which total approximately forty-five pages, begin with a summary of the attitudes of the KGB authorities towards the Vatican, representing it as an intensely hostile state that had waged an ideological war against socialism since the mid-nineteenth century and against the Soviet state since 1917. The major actions of the Catholic Church that endangered socialism included working against Soviet efforts in the Third World, particularly Latin America, and attempts to undermine the hold of socialism over the nations of Eastern Europe. Another frequent concern was the Vatican's use of "religious tourists" to settle into the satellite states and the Soviet Union itself to distribute "subversive" religious literature to Soviet citizens and allow them to send messages to hostile émigré organizations in the West.

The next section of the archive analyzes how the "Chekist organs" infiltrated numerous religious groups in Leningrad and Tolyatti. These groups had received religious and émigré literature from tourists, which was reproduced through *samizdat* and distributed to friends and family members.[59] Many of these "tourists" were prominent medical and scientific personnel. According to Mitrokhin's transcriptions, the KGB was eventually successful in turning a few members of these groups against the others, often using compromising materials on them or their family members; these subversive groups were eventually broken up during the late 1960s and early 1970s.

The borderlands between the Byelorussian and Ukrainian SSRs and the People's Republic of Poland were also viewed as a danger zone by Moscow in terms of the influence of the Vatican. The KGB noted that Polish Catholic priests often infiltrated into the Byelorussian SSR to serve as parish priests and engage in "counter-revolutionary propaganda," noting that "every third Catholic priest in the Byelorussian SSR is a Pole, and none of them can be trusted." More broadly, the Soviet regime tended to view Catholic churches

---

that these KGB agents had little influence on the direction of Vatican policy, although, as historian John Koehler also mentioned, they were successful in bugging the office of Cardinal Agostino Casaroli, one of the chief Vatican diplomats in charge of *Ostpolitik* in the 1960s and 1970s.

59. Literally "self-published," *samizdat* came to be known as the underground press of the USSR, as dissidents and human rights activists printed and distributed banned literature, using whatever methods and materials they had.

in the Soviet Union and satellite states—particularly the underground Eastern Rite Churches—with greater hostility than they had for the Vatican itself, even though they simultaneously argued that the actions of these churches were dictated by authorities in Rome. For example, the Catholic Church in the Lithuanian SSR—despite its professions of loyalty to the Soviet regime—remained a center for Lithuanian nationalism and was one of the primary barriers to Russification policies that had been implemented since 1945. The report mentions how priests and, occasionally, bishops passed on information to tourists about the persecution of religious institutions under communism. There are also some memorable quotes from Lithuanian clergy, such as Bishop Starkus, who bluntly stated that he would "only support Soviet authority when all Communists become religious believers." And yet, the KGB report makes it clear that in their eyes, these obstinate activities were undertaken as part of the Vatican's long-term plans of weakening Soviet authority.

The report also notes, more optimistically, that the KGB had been successful in recruiting some Lithuanian clergy to their ranks and had sent them abroad to engage in infiltration activities of their own. For example, the report noted that several KGB assets in the Lithuanian clergy traveled to Rome for the Second Session of the Twenty-first Ecumenical Council from September 29, 1963 to December 4, 1963. Their primary goal was to prevent Lithuanian émigré clergy from playing any role in the Council, particularly by stopping them from presenting themselves as legitimate representatives of the Catholic Church in Lithuania and forming connections with other reformist and "progressive" circles in the Vatican. In keeping with historical research on the Baltic republics, the KGB report notes that the social environment was one of the most troublesome ones for Moscow. The report on one uprising mentions acts of sabotage at the Alitussk Meat Packing plant (which humorously noted that a large portrait of Brezhnev had been defaced with the words: "Get Meat From This Pig!") and assassination attempts against party officials in Kaunas and Vilnius. The report concluded that these incidents had been instigated by former members of Lithuania's interwar Christian Democratic Party, now living in exile, who in turn were supported by "reactionary circles" in the Vatican.[60]

---

60. "Shifting the blame" for any problems under socialism onto hostile foreign powers is a recurring theme in Soviet archival documents, regardless of the historical era.

Nevertheless, the major issue between Moscow and the Vatican—at least in the eyes of the KGB—was the "organizational, material, and moral support to Uniates in Ukraine, orienting it towards supporting a nationalist mood among the population, with the view of constructing a revival of the Uniate Church in western regions of Ukraine." Of the many religious institutions that suffered persecution by the Soviet regime, few suffered as much as the estimated four million laity and clergy of the Byzantine (Eastern Rite) Catholic Church in the Ukraine following the end of the Second World War. The leader of the Byzantine Catholic Church in western Ukraine, where most Eastern Rite believers in the Soviet Union resided, was Archbishop Josyf Slipyj. Following his expulsion in 1963, Bishop Vasyl Velychovsky was placed in nominal control.

The KGB authorities were convinced that the Vatican and Slipyj were aggressively attempting to reestablish an Eastern Rite diocese in the western part of Ukraine, which could become a center for Ukrainian nationalist resistance to Moscow. In 1969, Yuri Andropov personally approved a program to discredit Velychovsky in Slipyj's eyes by publicly claiming that Velychovsky fully accepted the legitimacy of Soviet authority. The authors of the report boast that this led to Velychovsky being "thoroughly discredited" in Slipyj's eyes and, therefore, in the Vatican's eyes as well, although this was almost certainly overstating the case. Furthermore, KGB agents infiltrated religious institutions that Moscow believed supported subversive activity within Soviet borders, such as the Congregation on the Question of Eastern Churches, the Secretariat on Religious Affairs and Atheism, the Secretariat on Christian Unity, the Collegium Russicum, the Pontifical College of Saint Casimir, Saint Josaphat's Ukrainian Pontifical College, and the Ecumenical Center in Finland. These KGB actions were part of a broader plan to create "Catholic centers" in the Soviet Union, and possibly one day in the satellite states as well, that were fully independent of the Vatican's control and influence.

The next section of the Mitrokhin report discusses at length the recruitment of informers within the Eastern Rite religious community in the Ukrainian SSR, including someone who was recruited because the KGB agents falsely convinced him that his sister had been a KGB informer for years. In the western borderlands of the Lithuanian, Byelorussian, and Ukrainian SSRs, there were also frequent newspaper articles as well as radio broadcasts on the theme of "The Uniate Church—An Enemy to Peace and Progress." Much of the remainder of the report concerns KGB cooperation with the various secret police forces in the Soviet bloc to fight against the influence of the Vatican. Conferences involved members of the KGB and representatives of the Hungarian, Czechoslovak, or Polish security organs; occasionally, conferences involved all of them. Participants in these conferences expressed opinions about Vatican politics and the possible new directions of its foreign policy, its relationship with various socialist countries, negotiations of the Vatican with the Hungarian authorities, particular goals of the Vatican, intelligence work against the Vatican in a number of countries (including Italy, France, Austria, and Belgium), methods of placing agents within the churches, and joint activities against the Vatican (exchange of information and introduction of joint active measures). The KGB report acknowledged that their experts on religious policy tended to be drawn from the countries of Eastern Europe with large Catholic populations, which implied a strong reliance on Budapest, Warsaw and, to a lesser extent, Prague.

In the mid-1970s, the KGB sent several of its agents to the Vatican. Among their code names were "Tourist," "Missionary," "Miloslavsky," "Albert," and "Fidelio." Their instructions were described as follows: "Attempt to compromise the activities of the Vatican and its abilities to inspire people, to bring about divisions within the Vatican and also between the Vatican and capitalist countries, to strengthen the internal crisis in the Catholic Church which has grown since 1965, and to create opposition movements in the Church." The major conference on the theme of blocking the influence of the Vatican took place in February 1975 in Warsaw, with representatives of state security organizations from the USSR, Bulgaria, East Germany, Hungary, Poland, Czechoslovakia, and Cuba. They devised a plan to establish greater coordination among various Communist intelligence agencies in their efforts against the Vatican, using agents placed in the Vatican and church circles. In addition to the usual plans for placing or recruiting agents, one specific policy announced at the conference was to obtain and publicize as widely as possible material regarding connections between the Vatican and the Fascist governments in Italy, Germany, Spain, Portugal, and reactionary regimes in Latin America and Africa. Another goal was to block Vatican radio broadcasts into Russia. Simultaneously, and somewhat paradoxically, the conference noted that the foreign policy of Pope Paul VI had been far less dangerous and reactionary than that of many of his predecessors, and another long-term goal would be to help ensure that his successor continued with these policies of "peaceful coexistence." One means of promoting that end was to make an aggressive push to recruit both Vatican emissaries to socialist countries and students at the Pontifical Lateran University, particularly those who were training for work in the Vatican Diplomatic Corps.

By the late 1970s, the KGB was collaborating closely with the Polish security services regarding religious life and policy towards the Vatican, during a time when Poland's social, political, and economic situation became increasingly unstable. The report noted that over 800 members of Polish security organizations worked as agents within religious institutions in Poland, augmented by several Soviet citizens of Polish ancestry who had been sent there to engage in this work as part of a secret agreement between Warsaw and Moscow. In addition, there were occasional "religious conferences" designed to promote alternate perspectives to that of the "reactionary clique" of the Vatican; these were sponsored by the Central Committee's Church Commission on International Affairs. One of the most remarkable was from June 6–10, 1977 in Moscow, with the theme "Religious activities for creating a secure peace, disarmament, and the improvement of relations between nations." This conference was conceived as propaganda for the peace-loving Soviet Union, and to expose Western propaganda on the lack of religious freedom. The conference included over 500 foreign religious believers from various religious faiths. According to the KGB report,

> The Conference strengthened the authority of the Russian Orthodox Church in the international arena, to prevent efforts of foreigners and hostile elements in the Soviet Union to use the conference for negative actions against the USSR, and most importantly that the Vatican itself was deprived of the possibility of using its initiative with regards to religious life under socialism, and this demonstrated the lie of the lack of religious freedom.[61]

Another widely shared historiographical belief, that the Soviet government, particularly the KGB, viewed the election of Krakow archbishop Karol

---

61. The KGB considered the active participation of the Russian Orthodox Church in the World Council of Churches as a useful asset.

Wojtyła as Pope John Paul II as a particularly dangerous threat—not just to the Communist regime in Poland but to the entire Soviet bloc—is largely borne out by Mitrokhin's collection. Simultaneously, both Soviet and Polish security services considered the election of a Polish pope as a unique opportunity as well. On June 16, 1980, the head of KGB operations in Poland received a telegram from "the Center" (an informal nickname for KGB headquarters in Moscow), informing him that their mutual Polish "friends" in the Security Services (*Sluzba Bezpieczeństwa*, SB) suggested a major operative mission to place agents of Polish background in the Vatican to gain personal connections to Pope John Paul II. The long-term goals, the telegram said, were to reduce international tensions, promote peaceful coexistence and cooperation between governments, and influence the direction of Vatican policy.

"Influence" included the deepening of the schism between the Vatican and the USA, Israel, and other countries; increasing internal schisms within the Vatican; and implementing measures to prevent the strengthening of monasteries and religious institutions in socialist countries. Such influence might be exerted by using KGB contacts in the Russian Orthodox Church, as well as the Greek and the Armenian-Gregorian churches, for intelligence work, and by preventing any communication between these contacts and the Vatican that was not approved by the KGB.

Nevertheless, as the report subsequently stated, "With the election of John Paul II to the Holy Throne, the Vatican has openly engaged on the path of support of world imperialism and the ideological and political fight between East and West. The task of the Vatican is to divide socialism from the inside, and John Paul II has pursued these policies more intently than anyone in the Vatican since Pius XII." That being said, the report ended on a humorous note, as Mitrokhin's concluding section discusses a series of jokes made by KGB operatives regarding the Polish situation. One joke mentioned how John Paul II visited the interior ministry headquarters in Warsaw to inform them that their most important task had just been fulfilled. Another stated that, following the election of John Paul II by the College of Cardinals on October 16, 1978, the smoke changed from black to white and then to red. Everyone was confused, the joke went on, until they realized that Karol Wojtyła had burned his red membership card in the Polish United Workers' Party.

Ultimately, Mitrokhin's record of KGB activities—including their policies toward the Catholic Church in general and the Vatican in particular—must be viewed with a great deal of caution, as historians do not have access to the original documents. The identification of several KGB spies and informers as well as their code names—in a concluding section that lists nearly all the historical figures discussed in the report—is an important asset for historians and political scientists studying Soviet religious policies. The records also supplement other primary sources on the religious policies of the secret police forces in the Soviet Union and its satellite states. These forces worked to end religious life within their borders and to combat religious institutions beyond the Iron Curtain, of which the Vatican was the clearest threat.

The KGB Against the Vatican

By Vasili Mitrokhin

Translator's note: Mitrokhin's writings are not transcriptions of individual KGB reports, but rather summaries of numerous documents he secretly transported to his home from the KGB archives. As such, they do not follow a consistent pattern with regard to chronology, geography, or topic.
—Sean Brennan

1.

Eleven religious sects operate in the Soviet Union; among them are the reactionary Catholic and the illegal Uniate Churches, which are subordinate to the Vatican. The anti-Soviet nature of the churches and the incompatibility of their beliefs with Marxist-Leninist ideology mandated that the organs of state security in the USSR put a stop to their activities. The Vatican is one of the main targets of observation and penetration by agents of the KGB.[1]

Since the 1960s, religious organizations in the Soviet Union have remained very active in spreading their influence and recruiting new members; this includes Catholic organizations with the full support of the Vatican. Recent social and political crises across the world have contributed to the growth in the strength of Communist ideas, in both national libera-

---

1. "Uniate" although increasingly seen as a derogatory term for Eastern Rite Catholic churches (also known as the Byzantine Rite or Greek Catholic churches), was the common term used in official Soviet documents, including those of the political police. The vast majority of Eastern Rite Catholics in the Soviet Union were from the Ukrainian Greek Catholic Church, formed in 1595–1596 at the Union of Brest, in an agreement between the Ruthenian Orthodox Church and the Vatican. Its later name was a legacy of its inclusion in the Habsburg Empire. A significant percentage of the Byzantine Catholics came under the rule of Austria following the partitions of Poland between 1772 and 1795, during which Austria annexed Galicia, with its Polish and Ukrainian populations. From 1918 to 1939, most Ukrainian Greek Catholic churches were in the Polish Second Republic, with a minority in the Ukrainian Soviet Socialist Republic. After 1945, the USSR also had a sizeable minority of Roman Catholics, most through the annexation of Lithuania and, to a lesser extent, in the western borderlands of the Byelorussian Soviet Socialist Republic.

tion and worker's movements, as has the success of the Soviet Union in economics, politics, and the international arena, but the Catholic Church has survived these developments, and remains influential. The activities of their religious organizations are deliberately enacted with the goal of preventing the spread of communist ideas, to distract workers in capitalist and developing countries from the fight for social progress, and to use ideological diversions to internally weaken the Soviet Union. Church members disseminate religious propaganda literature, extol Western forms of life, promote nationalistic feelings amid the populations of Soviet republics, and sow dissatisfaction among the Soviet people towards the Soviet and Party organs.

In truth, there exists another point of view in some segments of the Vatican regarding their policies, as it has recently agreed to normalize its political approach through its contacts in the population of the USSR, especially in contacts with the intelligentsia. This has been reflected in its radio programs, sponsorship of tourism, and avoiding the most vulgar anti-Soviet attacks and instead inspiring patriotic feelings among the Soviet people. It now avoids rousing critical and nationalistic moods, nor does it encourage the violation of Soviet laws, and refuses to declare Marxism to be anathema. Instead, the Vatican emphasizes the various mistaken positions of Marxist theory; in its criticism of socialist society, it now states it is not against Socialism as a system of organizing society, but rather attacking only the totalitarian nature of its form. The Vatican has dedicated a propaganda campaign towards the intelligentsia and scientific workers. The direction, implementation, and coordination of these policies was entrusted to the Undersecretary of State of the Vatican [Giovanni] Benelli.[2] These policies occupy a special place in the fight with atheism under the control of Andrew Varga, a member of the Jesuits (in 1971).[3] However, these more progressive opinions are usually ignored in most Vatican leadership circles.

---

2. Cardinal Giovanni Benelli (1902–1981), originally from Tuscany, was a veteran clerical diplomat and a particularly critical figure in the Vatican's Foreign Policy from 1967 to 1977, and an early supporter of the Vatican's *Ostpolitik* of engagement with Communist regimes. He was also a close collaborator with Paul VI.

3. Reverend Andrew Varga, referred to by Mitrokhin by the Hungarian version of his name, Andreas, was the Superior of the Dispersed Hungarian Province of the Jesuits from 1955 to 1965; he would later work for the Vatican in the capacity described by Mitrokhin, and served as a professor of theology at Fordham University, the Jesuit university in New York City, from 1955 to 1988.

Internationally, Catholicism remains a political and ideological force that advocates for the rotting imperialist system. Representatives of the Vatican in the Congo endeavored quickly and decisively with the Belgian colonists to eliminate the leader of the Congolese people Patrice Lumumba.[4] The KGB, in 1961, was determined to make the world aware of this situation, making it clear that these reactionary actions were due to the efforts of the Vatican to strengthen its international position, emphasizing its authority and influence over the mass of believers and its desire to prevent any internal opposition by the clergy and laity to its policies. The KGB continues to expose the Vatican's use of capitalist resources in support of their activities against the Soviet Union and all other socialist countries.

The Vatican makes use of the so-called "tourist belief." Catholic agents work to involve believers into church life, which tears away workers from productive labor, and drives them to engage in oppositional activity against the Party and the State in socialist countries. It also advises believers not to read Soviet books and newspapers, not to attend the theatre, not to be tricked by the influence of atheism. In rural areas, Catholics create obstacles to the transmission of Marxist-Leninist ideology, buy up sporting-goods inventories and musical instruments for children, and work to influence technical and cultural circles. With the assistance of these measures, Catholic parishes direct children to deepen their religious beliefs, to divert the attention of children away from school education, from children's organizations, from Marxism-Leninism, and from military training.[5]

Service in the Vatican holds little attraction for priests who raise doubts about its teachings, while the Church believes that their service is already very important with regards to influencing the masses. Under the directives of the Vatican, churches recommend that clergy direct students to different areas of study with the goal of directing them towards a religious ideology, and to engage in Catholic propaganda to promote the popularity of the Vatican and hostility towards socialist countries, and to prepare future clergy

---

4. Lumumba was assassinated on January 17, 1961.
5. One characteristic of Soviet life, from 1917 to at least 1987, was that all foreigners in the country were viewed with distrust and suspicion by the regime. When they were not seen as actual spies of hostile foreign powers, including the Vatican, then they were viewed as people who brought subversive ideas and beliefs that could infect those who lived under Soviet rule. Arguably, this was partially a legacy of Tsarist times.

in coordination with secular institutions of higher education. The Catholic Church in the USSR has not entered any kind of agreement with the authorities, in contrast with the actions of the Orthodox Church.

Foreigners, through their contacts with Soviet citizens, attempt to provide them with illegal subversive literature, and have them pass it on to others. A graduate student at Leningrad State University, Tatiana Chizhevskaia (teacher of Russian language at the American Intelligence School), a citizen of the USA, distributed religious literature to Soviet Catholics. Following his entrance into the Soviet Union, Peter Moternach Boniface from the Vatican's Chevetogne Monastery in Belgium, often displayed interest in distributing Russian-language religious literature from the Vatican as well as other prohibited literature in the USSR.[6] Among the books that have been introduced and broadly distributed among readers in the USSR are "Solutions for Life's Problems" and "What is the Truth?" by the Catholic monk Fernand Lelotte; "Truth Seeker's Companion," by a Catholic priest named Pierre Teilhard de Chardin; "The Portrait of America," by a Catholic priest Raymond Leopold Bruckberger; "My Mission in Siberia," from the Archimandrite of the White Emigres Spiridon;[7] Mikhail Polsky's "New Martyrs and Confessors of Russia," Aleksandr Vetrov's "The Church in Bondage," and the works of Bulgakov and Berdiaev. The reading public has revealed a broad interest in these and other anti-Soviet religious books.[8]

The KGB in the city of Leningrad and the Leningrad Region, while observing the behavior of foreigners during their visits to churches, identified indi-

---

6. The Chevetogne Abbey is in the municipality of Ciney, in the province of Namur, located southeast of Brussels. Founded in 1925, it was unique in having chapels that accommodated monks from both the Western and Eastern rites, including some who were émigrés from the Soviet Union.

7. Archimandrite, a term used in both the Eastern Orthodox and Eastern Rite Catholic churches, can be roughly translated as "superior abbot" or "head abbot." The "White Émigrés" refers to those who were part of, or descended from, those who fought against the Bolsheviks during the Russian Civil War of 1918–1921. Fernand Lelotte was a Belgian Catholic theologian, while De Chardin and Bruckberger were both French Catholic theologians. Bruckberger was a Dominican who was originally of Austrian ancestry and De Chardin was a member of the Jesuit order.

8. Archpriest Mikhail Polsky, a cleric of the Russian Orthodox Church was imprisoned in the Solovetsky Monastery, the first facility of the Gulag, from 1923 to 1927 for

viduals who received such literature. Among Soviet citizens we have observed meet with these foreigners are the priest Troitsky from the Vladimir Cathedral, a member of the Institute for Theoretical Astronomy, Kazimirchak-Polonskaia, Doctor Panasov, a specialist in homeopathic medicine, lawyer Kasatkin, Associate Professor Rydanovskaia-Volkov, Deacon Rakov, bookbinder Fain, and others. These people received, made copies of, and then distributed similar kinds of literature. The KGB has also conducted several measures with our agents, where some of our own foreign agents were engaged in exposing this activity, such as a worker in a radio station in Monte Carlo (Monaco), Nikolai Peisti, Justin Mohrbacher (an American), and some others.

In the past, Kazimirchak-Polonskaia appeared to be an active participant in the Russian Student Christian Movement (RSXD).[9] She attempted to create an illegal religious organization Brotherhood, which was connected to the RSXD in the United States, France, Poland, and Czechoslo-

---

opposition to the Soviet regime, ultimately escaping to Iran in 1930 and chronicling the persecution of Christians by the USSR, dying in San Francisco in 1956. Alexander Vetrov was the pen name of Gleb Alesandrovich Rahr, a Russian of Scandinavian ancestry whose family was expelled from the Soviet Union in 1924, two years after his birth. During his youth in Germany, he was active in the Russian Orthodox exile community and helped to found the National Alliance of Russian Solidarists, (NTS-*Narodno-trudovoy soyuz rossiyskikh solidaristov*) an anti-Bolshevik group of emigres from the former Russian empire. An advocate of the unification of the Russian Orthodox Church Abroad with that in the Soviet Union, Rahr wrote "The Church in Bondage" in 1954 to raise global awareness of the plight of the Russian Orthodox Church in the Soviet Union. He died in Berlin in 2006. "Bulgakov" is a reference to Russian writer Sergei Nikolaevich Bulgakov, the son of an Orthodox priest, and one of the most famous Russian Orthodox philosophers of the early twentieth century. An economist and social commentator as well, he was expelled from Soviet Russia on Lenin's orders in 1922, part of a larger post-Civil War purging of members of the intelligentsia whose views were incompatible with those of the regime. He is not to be confused with Mikhail Bulgakov, a writer of the Stalinist period, who was critical of Soviet society but sometimes found favor with Stalin. "Berdiaev" refers to Nikolai Aleksandrovich Berdiaev, a Ukrainian Christian philosopher famous for his writings on the nature of human freedom. He was also expelled from the USSR on Lenin's orders in 1922 on the notorious "philosopher ships," and died in exile in France in 1948.

9. The Russian Student Christian Movement (*Russkoe Studencheskoe Khristianskoe Dvizhenie*) was formed in Czechoslovakia in 1923 by White Russian émigrés, who strove to keep the intellectual and spiritual life of Russian Orthodox Christianity alive among the Russian émigré community in Europe and throughout the world. Up to 1991, they maintained clandestine contacts with religious believers in the USSR.

vakia. Her confederate Panasov recruited children to assist the priest Vladimirov in producing and distributing subversive religious literature. A doctor of homeopathic medicine named Bubnov and his son, an engineer at the Semi-Conductor Institute, also took part in their actions, as did the machinist Khrennikov and a female bookbinder named Steshin.

The Chekist organs had shut down similar groups that were engaged in oppositional activities. These actions appear in operational records with the titles "Pharisees," "Apologists," "Renegades," and others. The preventative work towards these groups has been made easier by the fact that, despite the strength of the fanaticism of religious believers, they have not been able to create political goals for their activities. Specialists who have engaged in this preventative work have created an accurate analysis of this literature from a political point of view. Some of the activities by church members have been conducted by certain circles of believers who are all well known to each other. In these cases, the KGB has carefully undertaken operations involving the recruitment of agents among them, as well as inserting operatives among them. The case called "Pharisees" involved believers of different social statuses and educational levels. Kazimirchak-Polonskaia, Panasov, and their confederates Beliaev, Zheludkov, Shlezinger, and others took part in these actions. The KGB's goal was to stop the production and distribution of harmful, illegal literature distributed by their organization "Brotherhood," which had been prepared by Kazimirchak-Polonskaia and Panasov through their contacts abroad. The journal *Leningradskaia Pravda* published an article by a former scholar of theology named Osipov, using material provided to him by the KGB. This article was a highly critical essay on the book "Solutions for Life's Problems" and the brochure "Evangelization by the Jesuits." These efforts familiarized the local clergy with the dangerous content of these foreign publications.

Kazimirchak-Polonskaia, a doctoral candidate in science, studied national economics as her main field of specialization. KGB agents who specialized in religious affairs exercised a great amount of influence over her, including undermining her trust in Panasov. By weakening their relationship, the KGB was able to prevent them from aiding another group of religious believers among the intelligentsia named "Theosoph," which created and distributed subversive religious literature. Through the efforts of the KGB, Agent "Ivanna" proposed to Kazimirchak-Polonskaia that the group "Theosoph" had failed and revealed Panasov's confession that she had acted carelessly in distributing religious literature, as well as suggesting to her that they were under the observation of the KGB for all of their actions.

In contrast to the religious group's false proposals and guesses, the agent argued facts, preventing Kazimirchak-Polonskaia from raising any doubts about their veracity. After verifying these arguments of "Ivanna," Kazimirchak-Polonskaia stopped confiding in Panasov and avoided meeting with her. Then, a woman named Beliaev, a member of the Mechanical Institute, attended a preventative meeting with the Communist Party Committee in the Institute, attended by various employees of government agencies who participated in the conversation with them. Following these events, the woman Beliaev exerted her influence over the male members of the organization and they stopped meeting with Panasov and Kazimirchak-Polonskaia. Due to the excellent job our agents did in this task, we disrupted the expansion of the illegal religious organization "Brotherhood." A KGB agent was later substituted for Kazimirchak-Polonskaia as a head of the Faculty of Atheism at one of the Institutes of Higher Learning, under the pretext of studying the history of the Russian Student Christian Movement.

Panasov, however, did not cease her activities producing and distributing books and meeting with foreigners. Then she was discredited in the press and in her place of work. The newspaper "Change" published an article entitled "The Crooked Dualism of the Mushroom" about the hostile essence of foreign religious organizations, and the reactionary anti-Soviet activities of Panasov, a doctor named Shlezinger, and a student at Leningrad State University named Griba, with evidence provided by other religious students at the school. According to the material in the articles, in March 1966 a large meeting occurred at the Fourth Homeopathic Polyclinic, in which the subversive activities of Doctor Panasov was denounced. The meeting decreed that Panasov had been warned and reprimanded, and if her actions were repeated it would be treated by the authorities as criminal acts towards the broader public.[10] In a later meeting with Agent "Ivanna," Panasov admitted that she was alone in her religious mission, and that she should abandon it and dedicate herself to her work. The KGB Agent suggested to Panasov that she should give a statement of remorse to the KGB. She decided to consider

---

10. Public humiliations at places of employment for those who had run afoul of Soviet authorities were a common tactic for exerting social control in the post-Stalinist USSR.

this proposal, which led to further meetings with the KGB to prevent any further subversive religious activities.

In February 1966, we received from Agent "Omega" a report which mentioned that two individuals named Shlakat and Kasatkin were engaged in distributing subversive literature of a religious and political nature and were interested in involving others in these efforts. E.V. Kasatkin, born in 1934, who received an education in Soviet law, worked as an assistant to the department of Mail Vehicles. S.A. Shlakat was an instructor of the English language at several secondary schools. Our operation regarding their activities was named "Apologet." Shlakat was well-acquainted with the lawyer Kasatkin, the doctor named Sorokin, and the artist named Burmeister-Grochalskaia. At the request of his associates, Shlakat during the years 1965 and 1966 produced on a machine typewriter books with religious themes, such as Fernand Lelotte's "Solutions to Life's Problems," Archimandrite Spiridon's "My Mission in Siberia," the writings of Father John of Kronstadt, and numerous writings by an unknown author under the title "Religion and Contemporary Consciousness."[11] The author of the last book utilized slanders of communist and Marxist philosophy. In addition to these individuals, others who took part in the distribution of religious literature included an associate professor at the Institute for Advanced Study named Doctor Rudanovkskaia-Volkov, artist Burmeister-Grochalskaia, Doctor Skirchailo, Deacon Rakov, Doctor Shlezinger. Fain completed the bookbinding and the printing.

These people included many from the intelligentsia but, based on our knowledge, they did not try to incite people against the authorities. Because of this, the KGB decided not to classify them as having a criminal responsibility. For our agents to decipher and legalize the evidence concerning the illegal sources, a plan was developed to "accidentally" expose the group. Technical operatives confirmed that Kasatkin traveled to Moscow in a postal car with some copies of the first edition of the work "Religion in Cotemporary Consciousness." An operative was able to establish contact with the head of

---

11. John of Kronstadt (1829–1908) was among the most famous Orthodox clergy in Russia during the nineteenth and early twentieth centuries, famous for his reputed miraculous powers. Assigned to the parish of Saint Andrew's Church in Kronstadt, a naval base near Saint Petersburg, he was famous for his work with the urban poor, his long feud with Leo Tolstoy, and, towards the end of his life, his fierce anticommunism and monarchism.

Linear Services of the OUP,[12] Titov, a pensioner from the organs of the KGB, who provided to him the task in accordance with departmental instructions to jointly examine the personal belongings of each member of the postal delivery brigades. We discovered on Kasatkin six copies of the aforementioned books. The books were transferred to the KGB. Kasatkin was summoned by the KGB where, after a brief interrogation, he admitted that he assisted Shlakat in distributing "particularly ideological literature" and recognized his activities as harmful towards Soviet society. Kasatkin's statement was used in our interrogation of Shlakat, which revealed other participants who eagerly distributed religious literature such as Sorokin, Shlezinger, and Burmeister-Grochalskaia. Our agent-operatives conducted this mission legally and received official sanction for it. All these people involved in the distribution of the literature were brought into custody by the KGB, where they admitted to engaging in these activities. On them were discovered ten copies of Lelotte's books, and 30 copies of other harmful literature. All the subversive literature in this locality was confiscated by our agents.[13]

Over 300 members of the Department of Mail Deliverers on the October Iron Road attended the public censure of Kasatkin, including representatives from the Regional Party Committee, correspondents from the newspaper *Leningradskaia Pravda*, members of the Museum of Religion and Atheism, professional union activists, machinists, etc. Those at the assembly provided a harsh judgment on Kasatkin's activities, as they publicly rebuked him and simultaneously sent a letter to the rector of LGU calling for the revocation of his law degree, and stating that his activities dishonored his educational background at Leningrad State University, where he had studied Marxist-Leninist philosophy.[14]

---

12. The General Directorate of Post (OUP-*Obshei Upravelennie Pochta*), a branch of the Soviet Ministry of Communication, oversaw all mail delivery in the USSR.

13. As historians such as Maria Rogacheva and Simon Ings have pointed out, the Soviet scientific, medical, and engineering establishment had certain material privileges due to their service for the regime, but with this came greater scrutiny by the Soviet political police.

14. Leningrad, known before 1924 and since 1994 as Saint Petersburg, was Tsarist Russia's "Window to the West," and, with its proximity to neutral Finland, was seen as perhaps the most cosmopolitan city in Russia, by Soviet standards. Periodically, the city suffered through repressive measures by the KGB, due to its suspect intellectual climate. The "Leningrad Affair" in the late 1940s is the most notorious example.

Other participants in these subversive activities were also condemned, by a series of public judgements by their comrades, which were announced at a general assembly held at the Institute for Advanced Medical Training, located in the Botkin City Hospital of Leningrad. The Supreme Council of Religious Affairs also prevented further subversive religious activities by Deacon Rakov. *Leningradskaia Pravda* published an article in support of the KGB's actions titled "The Hermits," which described how the destruction of comradely spirit under socialism could be caused by some comrades coming under the influence of a foreign ideology.

The KGB decided to expose the priest Vladimirov to public criticism regarding his collusion with these other people. In the legal proceedings against him, KGB agents charged him with preparing typewritten texts of these subversive religious materials, and then giving them to the bookbinder Steshin, who in turn brought them to the institute. The typewritten texts of the book were then "accidentally" discovered by a vigilant Soviet citizen (in reality an agent of the KGB), who then reported their existence to the authorities. Under questioning, Steshin named to the KGB those already known as participants in the distribution of this literature, such as the machinist Khrennikov, Doctor Bubnov, and the priest Vladimirov. The KGB also received written confessions from them. They were also included in the union assembly to be publicly judged and criticized by their comrades in their place of work. Vladimirov's behavior was separately brought under investigation by the Supreme Council on Religious Affairs, which the religious hierarchy reported to.[15] The Council of the Leningrad Diocese discussed the behavior of Vladimirov, and its decision was to ban him from further spiritual activity as a penalty for distributing religious literature from abroad. As a result of these measures by the KGB, religious believers have become afraid, and have become more reluctant to deal with foreigners and religious literature.[16]

---

15. This section probably refers to a priest from the Russian Orthodox Church, as there was no "Leningrad Diocese" for the Roman Catholic Church during Soviet times. Leningrad's one large Catholic Church, the Church of Saint Catherine, had been closed on Stalin's orders in 1938. It had been part of the diocese of Mogilev, which had been the official Latin Rite diocese for the western regions of the Russian Empire since 1772.

16. The Supreme Council on Religious Affairs was the product of a 1965 merger between the Council on Russian Orthodox Church Affairs and the Council on the Affairs of Religious Sects, both creations (in 1943 and 1944, respectively) of Stalin's

The KGB has devoted its attention to the activities of foreign ideological centers, including two located in Sweden: the Slavic Mission's Religious Center and the Russian Biblical Correspondence Course. According to our analysis, much of the subversive religious literature that has been discovered in the USSR has come from these two locations. In 1967, two Swedish nationals, Persson Vengt and Khek Margaret, were found in Soviet territory with a Soviet typewriter and 300 copies of different kinds of religious literature, all translated into Russian. In July of the same year, the Swede Khaldorf was found with over 400 editions of religious literature. Other Swedes have been discovered attempting to distribute religious literature in the USSR. The Swedes' goods are distributed in double-bottomed suitcases, in overcoat arms, and in fuel canisters. The activities of these Swedish "tourists" was discussed in an article in *Leningradskaia Pravda* entitled "Undercover Evangelists."[17]

2.

Soviet industrial specialists from the city of Tolyatti left for specialized training and to receive equipment in Italy.[18] In this Soviet region, there were kiosks that specialized in selling Italian and foreign publications translated into Russian, including the works of Sinyavsky, Daniel, Pasternak (including *Doctor Zhivago*), and many others.[19] The population of Tolyatti has demonstrated

---

limited concessions to the Russian Orthodox Church and other religious institutions during the Second World War. Although intended to serve as a go-between for the Soviet government and various religious institutions, it often cooperated with the Institute of Scientific Atheism to promote atheistic policies. Although it was a part of the Soviet Council of Ministers, its leaders did not have ministerial rank. The Chair from 1960 to 1985 was Vladimir Kuroyedov.

17. Sweden was a neutral country in the Cold War, but much like Switzerland and Austria, its neutrality leaned towards Western political, economic, and military alliances. Swedish visitors were seen by the KGB as being little different than those from the United States, the United Kingdom, or West Germany—in other words, as potential spies or, at the very least, promoters of subversive literature.

18. Until 1964, Tolyatti was known as Stavropol na Volge (Stavropol on the Volga), located in the southeastern section of the European part of the RSFSR. It was renamed Tolyatti in 1964 in honor of the long serving General Secretary of the Italian Communist Party, Palmiro Togliatti. Throughout the Soviet period, many Italian Communists lived and studied there.

19. Boris Pasternak's "Doctor Zhivago" was published first in Italy in 1957. Despite winning the Nobel Prize for Literature and being widely regarded as one of the great

hostile, and even treasonous sentiments towards the Soviet regime, demonstrated by the widespread dissemination of literature attacking the government. 200,000 people live in the city, of which 50,000 live in dormitories, which recently have been fraught with massive disorder. Fights have broken out among workers, young students, and soldiers, in the process creating several hostile groups. Hostile foreign governments have sent their own agents, including a number of foreign specialists, and have managed to evaluate the situation in the city, identifying vulnerable areas in their attempts to undermine the Soviet order. The Vatican in particular has made active use of these specialists. In response, the KGB branch for the city of Tolyatti has requested from the Fifth Department of the KGB for the Kubyshev Region special assistance, in the form of additional agents to work among the Catholic population of the city, and to enlarge the district department. This assignment will be placed under the vigilant command of Lieutenant Colonel V.E. Kozhemyakin, head of the KGB Department in the city of Tolyatti.[20]

In Byelorussia, in 1970, there are 380 Orthodox Churches and 106 Catholic Churches. The Vatican and the Polish episcopate have striven to strengthen and spread Catholicism throughout the Byelorussian Soviet Republic. In much of the republic, the clerical administration for the Church is not legally organized; thus, in local areas, it has been filled by an illegal, unofficial administration under the control of the Vatican and Cardinal Wyszyński of the Polish People's Republic.[21] Nearly all the priests serving there

---

novels of the 20th century, its mixed view on the Russian Revolution and the rise of Bolshevism led to its being banned in the USSR until 1987. Pasternak was forced to turn down an invitation to Stockholm to receive the Nobel Prize. "Daniel" and "Sinyavsky" refers to Russian writers Yuli Daniel and Andrei Sinyavsky, who had been tried and convicted of writing and distributing "anti-Soviet literature" in 1965. Their works, like Pasternak's, were banned until the late 1980s, although they were distributed in the underground press, nicknamed *samizdat* (roughly "self-published). The trial of Daniel and Sinyavsky was widely seen as the beginning of Brezhnev's Neo-Stalinist policies, and as the impetus for the Russian dissident movement.

20. The "Fifth Department" of the KGB is a shorthand reference to the Fifth Chief Directorate, created in 1969, which attempted to control religious activity in the USSR in coordination with the Council of Religious Sects, as part of its overall mission to crush any kind of dissent.

21. Cardinal Stefan Wyszyński was the Archbishop of Warsaw from 1948 to 1981. In 1953, he was arrested and imprisoned by Poland's Stalinist government for supporting the anticommunist resistance in the country, then placed under house arrest until

are well known as fanatics and obscurantists. The creation of an official Catholic clerical administration in the Byelorussian SSR would bring them even further under the influence of the Vatican and the Polish Episcopate. Polish citizens in their letters to relatives and friends in the Belarussian SSR interpret events in the Polish People's Republic (PPR), such as the shootings in Gdansk, with a politically harmful, anti-Socialist attitude, and many letters have a clear intention of instigating hostile behavior among Soviet citizens in the Byelorussian SSR.[22] In October 1970, in the village of Zarenchanka, located the Grodnensky Region, a Catholic church was closed under the orders of the local authorities. In the following days, nearly all of the population failed to attend work at the collective farm and were strongly and publicly indignant at the closing of the church. An analogous situation also occurred in the village of Novaia Ruda, located in the same region. It was marked by the refusal of different groups to work, violation of labor discipline, and attempts at massive upheaval. Sixty-eight churches are in the Grodnensky region, and every fourth inhabitant of the region is Catholic. Almost 50% of those involved in these protests served time in prison. To respond to these situations, the KGB had at its disposal a sufficient number of agents, who immediately received information about these actions of the Catholic clergy and their followers.

In March of 1967, the Ministry of Foreign Affairs of the USSR presented a number of questions to the KGB. The deputy chairman of the KGB, C. Bannikov, responded on April 4, 1967 in a letter to Deputy Minister of Foreign Affairs S. P. Kozirev. In the letter, the KGB advised against restoring bishops Sladkiavichus, Stepanovich, and Dyulbinsky to their clerical offices, as returning them to their work in leadership positions in the Church would create a clear political threat to the Soviet government, especially in relation

---

1956. Following his release, he successfully negotiated with Poland's newly appointed Communist leader Władysław Gomułka for greater freedom of action for the Catholic Church in Poland than for any other religious institution in the socialist world. Nicknamed "the uncrowned king of Poland," he later served as a mentor to Karol Wojtyła. Wyszyński remained a subtle but firm opponent of Communism and was viewed with continual suspicion by Moscow.

22. "The shootings in Gdansk" refers to the large demonstrations in that Polish city against Władysław Gomułka's rule in December 1970, which were violently suppressed by the police, killing dozens. These shootings led to Gomułka's resignation as General Secretary of the Polish United Workers Party. He was replaced by Edvard Jierek, who ruled through the bulk of the 1970s.

to the religious unity of the country. It would also encourage more hostile activities from the reactionary part of the Catholic clergy and nationalist elements and, in turn, might incite Catholics in Byelorussia to undermine Soviet government policies. The most important goal is to prevent the creation of an anti-Soviet position by the institutional Church. Bishop Skladkiavichyus was eventually appointed without the agreement of the government of the Byelorussian SSR.

The Vatican does not formally recognize the apostolic administration in Moscow and other areas in the USSR, on account of the small number of Catholics in these regions of the country.[23]

Questions concerning the organization of the Church hierarchy in Byelorussia and the assignment of Cardinal Cherniavsky as its leader were not resolved, although there remained the possibility that his position in the Catholic Church hierarchy would be reexamined at a better time.

In 1982, the first secretary of the Grodnensky Regional Committee of the Communist Party of the Byelorussian SSR wrote an essay that was published in *Chronicle of the KGB* Number 95. This essay cited two proposals of the Central Committee of the Communist Party of the Soviet Union: "Concerning Measures to Further Strengthen the Political Vigilance of the Soviet People" from May 23, 1977, and "Concerning Measures to Increase Political Vigilance in the Interest of Strengthening the Security of State Borders of the USSR" from June 28, 1977. The essay provided the following description:

> The Grodnensky Region is located on the border with Poland. The inhabitants in the region were aware of events in the Polish People's Republic, through Polish newspapers, radio, and television, and through letters and personal acquaintances. Events in Poland have contributed to the creation of a negative mood in the population towards the regime and have reawakened feelings of nationalism. Thus, it has become necessary to

---

23. Given that the Ukrainian Greek Catholic Church had been effectively forced underground in 1946, and the Diocese of Mogilev—besides the western parts of Byelorussia—increasingly existed only on paper after the late 1930s, the only part of the Soviet Union where a clear episcopal structure existed for the Roman Catholic Church was in the Baltic republics, especially Lithuania.

engage in serious counter-propaganda amongst the population. Everyone is aware of the events occurring in the worker's collectives, and the events that occurred in their homeland.[24]

One hundred religious communities are in the region, including sixty-five Catholic Churches. Prominent members of the clergy and the laity continue to attempt to organize local children in religious life, to extend greater influence over them. Many Catholics are attempting to revive dangerous beliefs concerning the inseparability of the Polish nation and the Catholic Church; one of the ideas inherent in these beliefs is that every Byelorussian Catholic is really a Pole.[25] The Vatican and the Polish episcopate continue to use their influence over believers to control the activities of Catholic organizations in the Grodnensky region. This influence has significantly increased since the election of the Polish Bishop Wojtyła to lead the Roman Catholic Church. Religious literature from abroad is continually distributed with the intention of strengthening religious communities, emissaries have snuck information into the Grodnensky region informing religious believers about the situation of their fellow Catholics in other countries. None of this has occurred without our awareness. For example, the KGB has successfully halted frequent attempts by certain religious fanatics to register new members in churches or in secret cultist meeting places.

In May 1979 and January 1980, the Central Committee of the Communist Party of Byelorussia organized seminars in Grodno for atheist propagandists. During the seminars, they analyzed a report from the Party's Regional Committee entitled "Concerning the Work of Party and Social Organizations of the Grodnensky Region for the Promotion of Atheist Education in the Population with regards to the Vatican's attempts to revive its Influence over Catholics in Socialist Countries." Party workers from

---

24. "The events" referred to the Solidarity crisis in Poland from 1979 to 1981, which shook the Communist regime in Poland to its core and was the biggest crisis in the Soviet bloc since the Prague Spring in 1968. The Grodnensky Region is referred to in modern-day Belarus as the Hrodna region, which is in western Belarus, with the Minsk district to its east and both Poland and Lithuania to its west.

25. As this observation in the report reveals, pre-revolutionary ethnic, religious, and national issues of the former Russian Empire occasionally broke through the Marxist-Leninist straitjacket in the Soviet Union.

Moscow, Kiev, Minsk, the Supreme Council of Religious Affairs, and a commission from the local Soviet all took part in these seminars.[26]

Party leaders taught the seminar participants about promoting a sense of patriotism and citizenship in the population. There were also speeches about the need to continue the fight against religion. The seminar instructors also emphasized it was necessary to closely monitor people exiting and entering the regions on the Soviet borders, especially people susceptible to foreign influence.

3.

Lithuanian Nationalists consider their native language and their allegiance to the Catholic Church to be significant barriers against Russification. Priests in the past have engaged in anti-Soviet activities, but now present themselves as loyal. Nevertheless, they continue to engage in subversive, illegal activities, such as listening to Vatican Radio and Western radio stations to get news about international events. A priest named Talachka, while in a group of sympathetic priests, remarked, "In the contemporary situation, priests should be especially cautious, they should not attempt to unleash anti-Soviet feelings, in order to avoid acts of reprisals by the state. But this does not imply that priests should simply act passively. It is necessary to use diplomacy, engage in falsehoods and guile." Anti-Soviet sentiments regarding the situation in Lithuania have been propagated by the Vatican, by Lithuanian clergy, and by nationalist émigrés, creating among believers a dangerous combination of a nationalist mood and religious fanaticism.[27]

---

26. Minsk was the capital of the Byelorussian SSR and remains the capital of Belarus. Grodno, also referred to as Hrodna, is the largest city in western Belarus, located near the borders of both Poland and Lithuania. It was the capital of the Grodnensky Region.

27. Independent between the Soviet-Polish War and the Second World War, Lithuania was absorbed by the USSR in 1939, "liberated" by the Nazis in 1941, and reconquered by the Red Army from 1944 to 1945. A guerilla war between the Lithuanian Nationalist underground, known as the "Forest Brothers," and the combined strength of the Red Army and the KGB, dragged on into the early 1950s. The Lithuanian SSR was among the most troublesome for Moscow to control over the next four decades. Lithuania also had the largest percentage of Roman Catholics in the Soviet Union; the other two Baltic Republics, Estonia and Latvia, were largely Lutheran among their religious population.

Six hundred thirty churches are in Lithuania, divided into four dioceses, and staffed by 826 priests and six bishops. The major clerical seminary is in Kaunas, which is staffed by 33 clerics. The Catholic clergy are trained to have an irreconcilable position towards the politics of the Soviet government with regards to questions of religion, to win independence of the Church from control by the Soviet state, and to create opposition on the part of their parishioners towards socialism. Several priests from the diocese have frequently requested of the government to allow certain public religious activities and to increase the number of the clerical staff at the Kaunas seminary, and to repeal the regulations on the activities of priests set by the Council of Religious Affairs. In their sermons, the priests misrepresent the position of the churches, inform religious believers that the state is irretrievably hostile towards them, order believers to defend the freedom of their priests and bishops, emphasize that Soviet laws regarding religion have no legitimate authority, and state that the priests are victims who are unjustly persecuted by these laws. The priest Klimas among a circle of like-minded persons stated, "I am determined to inform the national masses about the factual situation of the churches. The people will not allow the churches to be destroyed. Soviet actions have brought about the moral degeneration of society, and it can only be revived through the efforts of the churches."

Priests frequently attempt to send across our borders information about the persecution of religion and clergy in Lithuania. These actions are often committed with the aid of tourists, or through postal channels from Tbilisi, Donetsk, Grodno, Frunze, and other cities of the Soviet Union. Priests also attempt to use illegal channels to send them abroad through Poland.[28] Inspired by the reactionary part of the Catholic clergy, Bishops Stonis and Starkus and some priests have appeared to refuse to perform their state-mandated functions. Starkus in a meeting with his staff declared, "I will be loyal to Soviet authority only when all Communists become religious believers."

The KGB has striven to isolate the reactionary priests from taking an active part in religious life in Lithuania. This has been necessary because

---

28. Tbilisi, also known as Tiflis, was the capital of the Georgian SSR. Donetsk was the largest city in Eastern Ukraine. Frunze, currently named Bishkek, was the capital of the Kyrgyz SSR.

the Vatican has devoted considerable attention to Lithuania's internal affairs. On the fiftieth anniversary of Lithuania's declaration of independence, on February 16, 1968, the pope transmitted to the Lithuanian bourgeoisie worldwide congratulations on Vatican radio.[29] Vatican Radio and other foreign radio stations with anti-Soviet positions continue to distort religious life in Lithuania. The Vatican also continues to provide material support to the clergy.

Catholic clergy in the Lithuanian SSR had tried to establish illegal contacts with Lithuanian émigré priests, providing them with slanderous information about the position of the Catholic Church in Lithuania, through illegal channels of communication, such as intermediaries and false addresses in Poland. The priest Polukaitis, in an intercepted letter which he attempted to smuggle abroad, wrote: "desiring to keep on in life, I need to fight for every person on an individual level. The front of this battle becomes ever more difficult, the situation graver. However, abandoning this fight would be a disgrace, as this is a fight not for life, but to the death, until the final victory." In sermons and meetings with believers, concealed with religious phraseology, priests encourage the laity to believe the current situation cannot last forever, urging patience in maintaining their religious faith. These tactics have been successful in strengthening their influence over children and youth. In order to draw believers into the churches, the Catholic clergy devote great attention to various types of religious activities, regularly marked with sumptuous celebrations of religious holidays, organizing pilgrimages to holy sites, improving the music of Church services, attempting to organize the education of children in the catechism, arranging entertainments, enrolling youths in the Church choirs, exercising influence over the upbringing of the next generation through influencing their parents, and engaging in individual educational work.[30]

---

29. Lithuania had been part of the Russian Empire since the partitions of the Polish-Lithuanian Commonwealth in the late 18th century. Following the Russian Revolution, the State Council of Lithuania, whose members included four Catholic priests, announced the restoration of the country's independence at a conference in Vilnius, on the conference's opening day, February 16, 1918. Its independence lasted until 1940.

30. The relatively clear diocesan structure and freedom of action of the Lithuanian Catholic Church, although not as great as the freedom of the Catholic Church in Poland, was an anomaly in the Soviet Union, comparable only perhaps to the relative freedom granted to Muslim communities in Central Asia.

In the seminary, the number of students does not compensate for the number of priests who are retiring or dying, as the authorities can only enroll five students per year.[31] Many priests have thoughts of creating an underground Catholic Church, which would be staffed by illegal priests. The priests write memoirs, essays, and scientific works on theology for all clergy and believers; Catholic monks have made copies of these works on printing presses, printed as books and distributed throughout the religious community. The priest Markaitis condemned these religious allowances in an issue of *Highest Sower*, in the article "To Help Young Priests."

The College of Saint Casimir was created in Rome in 1945 to prepare priests for service in an independent Lithuania. In 1963, Prelate Tulaba, one of our agents, became its director; he was the former rector of the Vilnius Theological Seminary. Tulaba pretended to have an important role among Lithuanian clerical émigrés. In his work for the KGB, Tulaba was also engaged at the United Center for Catholic Action, located near Munich, which was created in 1967, as well as the Union of Lithuanian Priests, the Institute for Catholic History and Religious Culture in Italy, and the United American-Lithuanian Fund—this last of which, while ostensibly created to study religion, engages in many ideological diversions.

The Second Session of the 21st Ecumenical Council occurred from September 29 to December 4 1963 in Rome. Among those attending as part of the delegation of Lithuanian Catholic clergy:

- Agent "Azhuolas"—The leader of the delegation, head of the Kaunas and Vilkaviškis Archdiocese, Archbishop Stankevich
- Agent "Putinas"—Head of the Panevėžys and Kaišiadorys Diocese, Bishop Bakhis
- Agent "Gedeminas"—Head of the Vilnius Archdiocese, Archbishop Kirvaitis
- Agent "Saul"—Chancellor of the Vilkaviškis Archdiocese, the priest Krikshchy

---

31. This restriction mirrored religious policies in the other Soviet satellites. The state ordered the closing of seminaries, or at least strict limitations on how many students they could enroll—the idea being that the eventual lack of trained clergy would further the long-term goal of eradicating religious faith and institutions.

- Agent "Algis"—Chancellor of the Vilnius Archdiocese, the priest Mazheik
- Agent "Antanas"—Chancellor of the Panevėžys Diocese, the priest Prank

The KGB put before the delegation of our agents the following tasks:

- To seek permission to take an active part in the work of the Council;
- To prevent clerical émigrés from taking part in sessions organized by the Catholic Church.
- To receive from the Vatican an official recognition that the members of the delegation, not the émigrés, are the legal representatives of the Lithuanian clergy.
- To ignore the efforts by the College of Saint Casimir and other émigré centers.
- To refute statements by the clerical delegates about the existence of persecution of religious believers in the USSR.
- To fulfill other assignments given by the KGB.

The Presidium of the Central Committee of the Lithuanian Communist Party decided during this period to prepare tourist groups of Lithuanian Catholics, and arrange for them to travel to Rome for the Ecumenical Council. Among these groups were several agents of the KGB:

- "Prapas"—Aushrunas Alfonsas, son of Ignas, a medical student and member of the Institute of Hygiene and Epidemics in the city of Vilnius
- "Neman"—Gaiauskas Kostas, son of Antanas, abbot of the Church of Saint Theresa and Ostrobramska Kaplitz (The Shrine to the Lady of the Dawn), deacon of Vilnius Deaconate
- "Brunus"—Barauskas Brunus, son of Yurgis, chancellor of the Telšiai Curia
- "Gudrus"—Novelskis Bronyus, son of Yurgis, abbot of the Church in the city of Alitussk
- "Biarzhas"—Kuzmuitskas Yugris Kazisovich, abbot of the Rietavas Church, in the Kaunas Region
- "Domov"—Paberzhis Ignas, son of Ignas, abbot of the Trakai Church
- "Vaitekunas"—Kuchinas Povilas, son of Povilas, monsignor of the Church of Saint Anna in the city of Vilnius

- "Zubov"—Dakiniavichus Prapas, son of Vatzlovas, a member of the Republican Committee for the Defense of Peace, chief pharmacist in the city of Birštonas.

Among the leaders of the tourist group was the KGB agent "Labunas," whose real name was Matulaitis Iozas, son of Ionas, a prelate of the Holy See and professor at the Kaunas Spiritual Seminary. Another tourist leader was an operative of the KGB, Sunialaitis Antanas Antanovich, who worked as a legal consultant to the Vilnius Construction Trust.[32]

Other associates of the KGB included in a group were from the Simonaitis family.

The following tasks were put before the group:

- To strengthen the diplomatic position of the Lithuanian delegation, which are taking part in the Second Session of the Ecumenical Council.
- To meet with some visible representatives of the reformist circles in the Vatican.
- To attempt to have an audience with Pope Paul VI, and give him copies of the paintings of the Madonna of Ostra Brama (an amber mosaic) as a gift.

As a secondary note, "Azhuolas," an agent of the KGB, at the Second Session of the Ecumenical Council in Rome, conducted himself inappropriately, departing from the approved KGB line of action, causing a considerable amount of discord and unhappiness in the rest of the group, leading to his removal from activities as an agent.

The train ride across the Italian border was unusually eventful for our agents among the clergy. They were in a difficult situation, as officially they had to act as fighters for religious belief, trying to strengthen the influence of the Catholic Church. Meetings with priests from other countries were entirely different from meetings with each other, especially dealings with those who

---

32. Nearly all urban construction in the Soviet Union was done by large Construction Trusts that operated in all of the major cities, which were part of the Soviet State Committee for Construction or *Gosstroy*, an abbreviation of the title *Gosudarstvennoye Stroytelstvo* or State Construction.

worked in the Vatican itself. The situation instilled in our agents beliefs about the well-being of the churches in the West, about the possibility of increasing the number of seminarians and ascending the ranks of the clerical hierarchy in Lithuania, and about the hardness of the anti-Soviet positions of the Lithuanian clerical émigrés and the Vatican leaders. Because of challenges like these, only agents in whose reliability we are absolutely certain are sent abroad.[33] Agent "Hilvus," who held a leadership position in a diocese in Lithuania, while abroad devoted all of his efforts and attention to be ordained as a bishop. However, he was not ordained as one. When questioned by the KGB as to why this did not occur, he answered, "At home we serve one God, but in the Vatican, they have decided to serve another."

The Vatican considers the Lithuanian SSR to be one of the least loyal Soviet republics, considering the openly nationalistic views of the population, and its considerable discontent with the Soviet government, which has largely been organized by the Catholic Church. A clear indication of these attitudes, especially among young Lithuanians, was found in Kaunas, where in June 1973 a student named Kalanta committed an act self-immolation in the central square of the city, covering himself in gasoline and then igniting himself.[34] The authorities could not foresee and could not prevent such acts of protest in the city where, as in other satellite states, every inhabitant felt that the dignity of their nation had been assaulted. The Lithuanians have a national tradition of leaving flowers at the place of the death of a person. The authorities were aware that the usual kinds of demonstrations would occur, and that the city square would be swarmed by young Lithuanians. This necessitated that soldiers surround the square to prevent the laying of flowers. The soldiers' presence, however, did nothing but spur on the population of Kaunas. The parents of the deceased and the students who

---

33. This was also the case with Soviet scientists, artists, and athletes who were allowed to travel abroad. Some still defected to the West, of course.

34. This was one instance of a common form of protest in the late 1960s and early 1970s. In addition to the famous instances of the Buddhist monks in South Vietnam, three Czech university students in Prague—Jan Palach, Jan Zajic, and Evzen Plocek—committed suicide by self-immolation in January and February 1969, in protest against the Warsaw Pact invasion of Czechoslovakia four months before. The similar suicide of Romas Kalanta in Lithuania's second largest city, Kaunas, in May 1972 marked the beginning of a wave of nationalist-inspired protest against the Soviet regime. Twelve other Lithuanians followed Kalanta's example over the next few years.

studied with him began to throw flowers over the heads of the soldiers. The Red Army soldiers at the square, who were entirely Russian, removed the flowers from the square on the orders of their officers. An angry crowd responded by stomping the flowers at the Lenin memorial. The event had not been forgotten by the inhabitants of the city by 1976, as a commemoration of the student's death turned into a ceremony honoring the victims of the fight for national independence, which in turn was broken up by soldiers and police from the organs of state security.

The month of November 1975 in Vilnius concluded with the suicide of a young Lithuanian poet whose literary work expressed religious mysticism. His decision to commit suicide publicly revealed a desire to send out a nationalist message.

Lithuanian nationalists have also sympathized with Sakharov, who was in Vilnius in May 1976 to take part in a judicial proceeding concerning like-minded colleagues. There also exists sympathy for Solzhenitsyn.[35]

In April 1976 at the Alitussk Meat-Packing Plant, an act of sabotage occurred. This meat-packing plant was one that exported meat. A number of protests against the actions of the factory administrators took place; during one of these protests, a large group of strikers jammed the wheels of the trains with meat products from the factory. In nearby Kaunas, a portrait of Brezhnev was defaced with the words "Get Meat From This Pig." There were also several assassination attempts, which were undertaken by zealous nationalists led by Grishkevichus, directed at supporters of the Soviet government such as Snechkus.[36]

---

35. Andrei Sakharov and Aleksandr Solzhenitsyn were the two most prominent Russian dissidents in the Soviet Union. The atheist Sakharov, a nuclear physicist turned human rights activist, wanted the Soviet Union to enact Western-style economic and political reforms, while the devoutly Orthodox Solzhenitsyn longed for Russia's return to its pre-revolutionary social and cultural traditions. Solzhenitsyn served eight years in Soviet penal camps after making a comment critical of Stalin in a letter to a friend. This experience inspired his first successful novel, *A Day in the Life of Ivan Denisovich*, and many of his later writings.

36. Brezhnev's increasing vanity, marked by his habit of constantly awarding himself new medals, in combination with his pronounced physical deterioration, made him a figure of increasing ridicule throughout the Soviet Union. "Snechkus" refers to Antanas Iuzovich Snechkus, who had worked for Lithuania's Communist Party in the

The KGB has tried to orient some nationalists and religious followers toward supporting the idea of nuclear disarmament. A former leader of Lithuania's Christian Democratic Party, a publicist and doctor of science named Keliotis, returned to Lithuania following his imprisonment in the RSFSR. Upon his return, he reestablished connections with former bourgeois government functionaries and former members of the intelligentsia, engaged in correspondence with émigrés, and received from them literature and material assistance. In a brief amount of time, this group was able to surround itself with young members of the technical and scientific intelligentsia, over which they exercised a damaging influence. Keliotis' group turned them towards supporting Lithuanian nationalism, although some of these youths have also expressed approval of the achievements of the last few years. The solution our agents devised was to convince members of this group to condemn their past activities, to renounce their views and political activities, and to speak out openly against them in the press. This work went on for over two years, with constant attempts at ideological reeducation and at neutralizing the negative influence of émigré nationalists. Operatives who had direct contact with the group eventually strengthened their ideological influence over the young Lithuanian intelligentsia, having demonstrated that following our ideology contributed to the overcoming of material difficulties. In the case of Keliotis specifically, efforts to gain influence over him included increasing his KGB pensions, restoring compensation for his manuscript—which had been been confiscated upon his arrest—and providing him with continual translation work. As a result of these actions, Keliotis moved away from his concerns about promoting Lithuanian nationalism, and towards the idea of disarmament. In the newspaper article, "A Bridge, Which Still Does Not Exist," which contained an interview with him, he discussed attempts by émigrés to use cultural cooperation with the Lithuanian SSR for hostile purposes.

Similar measures were taken regarding five former authorities from bourgeois Lithuania.[37] Tishkus and Skaisgiris took part in counter-propaganda measures for the KGB.

---

interwar era and played an instrumental role in both 1940 and 1945 in imposing Soviet rule on Lithuania. The KGB was probably correct in believing he was despised by Lithuanian nationalists living in and outside of the country.

37. "Bourgeois Lithuania" is a sometimes-derogatory, Soviet-coined term. It refers to the time between 1920, when Lithuania and the other Baltic states achieved

Atheistic spectacles and effective public demonstrations were also held to weaken the Catholic Church. Given the impossibility of using agents drawn from the Lithuanian Catholic clergy, agent "Almov" resorted to harsher Chekist measures intended to draw people out of the Church.[38] At one church, in the presence of the believers, Almov strongly denounced spiritual titles, connecting them to the uselessness of the rituals themselves and the vestments of the clergy. He then spoke out against Catholicism in general, Vatican Radio, and the *samizdat* publication, "The Chronicles of the Catholic Church in Lithuania."

Another operative was Vytautas Alseika, who lived in America, worked in a Lithuanian Nationalist group abroad, and later was part of the Spiritual Committee of Liberation for Lithuania. He published an article in a collection entitled *Three Decades in Emigration*," published in 1977. This article used archival documents provided by our operatives, who had allowed Alseika to live legally abroad. These documents included material on the activities of opponents. The main purpose of the article was to promote military disarmament, driven by a recognition of the tragic results of military destruction in the past.[39]

---

independence; and 1940, when they were annexed by the Soviet Union. Philip Taubman, "In Lithuania, Too, Nationalism Surges," *The New York Times*, July 23, 1988, https://timesmachine.nytimes.com/timesmachine/1988/07/23/146888.html?pageNumber=3

38. "Cheka" is a rendering of the acronym for the Soviet political police's first name, the All-Russian Extraordinary Commission for Combating Counter-Revolution and Sabotage. It existed under this name from 1917 to 1922, then was renamed the GPU (the Main Political Directorate), before becoming the NKVD (the People's Commissariat of Internal Affairs) from 1934 to 1946, then the MVD (Ministry of Internal Affairs) from 1946 to 1954, and finally in 1954 the KGB (Committee for State Security). Despite these changes of name, agents of the KGB, several decades later, were still often referred to as Chekists by the Soviet population, and they often referred to themselves by this name as well.

39. Vytautus Alseika was, as the report indicates, a Lithuanian émigré journalist born in 1912 who spent much of the Cold War living abroad and working for Lithuanian émigré organizations, although he returned to Lithuania after it won its independence from the Soviet Union and died there in 2002. Penetrating anticommunist émigré organizations was one of the primary foreign objectives of the KGB, especially if those émigrés came from the Soviet Union itself.

4.

The Vatican provides organizational, material, and moral support to Uniates in the Ukraine, orienting it towards supporting a nationalist mood among the population, with the aim of reviving the Uniate Church in western regions of the Ukraine. Nationalists in western Ukraine have worked for the creation of a Kievan-Galician Archdiocese to be led by Cardinal Slipyj.[40] The Vatican helps the Uniates in the preparation of cadres in Rome for this secret work.

Vilkovsky, an illegal Uniate priest, was placed under observation by the KGB. In 1962, he met in his apartment with several tourist seminarians from abroad. In June of 1963, in the city of Kiev, a group of French tourists including a Jesuit priest named Konir, an agent of the Vatican, met with him. External observation revealed that, after a thorough check of his apartment for any surveillance equipment, Konir met with Vilkovsky there for twenty minutes.

On May 30, 1979, an Italian citizen named Bernardo Vincenzo was detained at the Soviet-Polish border, with more than 12,000 rubles he had failed to declare. Under interrogation, he admitted that the money was given to him by a priest named Ivan Ortinsky at a Greek Catholic church in Italy, for his sister, who lives in Lviv. Agents of the KGB were able to create a psychological portrait of Vincenzo, which included the following: Vincenzo valued the reputations of the Uniate priests and desired to increase his influence over them. He also feared any legal actions the Soviet authorities might take against him. Vincenzo may also have met with Bishop Fedoruk the former head of the Catholic monastery run by the Basilian order. Fedoruk is connected with the OUN (Organization of

---

40. Archbishop Josyf Slipyj became head of the Ukrainian Greek Catholic Church upon the death of Metropolitan Andrey Sheptytsky in 1944. For the false charge of collaborating with the Nazis during their occupation of the Ukraine, and for refusing to accept the fraudulent Synod of Lviv when the Soviet government, with the connivance of the Russian Orthodox Church, attempted to dissolve the Ukrainian Greek Catholic Church, Slipyj served almost eighteen years (1945 to 1963) in Soviet labor camps. Exiled by Nikita Khrushchev in 1963, Slipyj lived in Rome but maintained contacts with Ukrainian Greek Catholics in the USSR, which were forced to maintain an underground existence between 1946 and 1988.

Ukrainian Nationalists).[41] All of this information was used by the KGB to bring necessary pressure on Vincenzo. He acknowledged that he could get information from Ortinsky's sister concerning the illegal activities of the Basilian monastic order, and about the activities of Fedoruk. At the end of 1978, Ortinsky informed Vincenzo that Pope John Paul II expressed interest in the situation of Uniate priests in the USSR.

John Paul II subsequently met with Slipyj, to whom he suggested that the Uniate authorities petition the Soviet government to legalize their activities. For this endeavor to succeed, the pope needed more information about the state of the Uniate Church, including its numbers of clergy and believers, and he needed a means of receiving information consistently about their activities. He hoped that Fedoruk would become his information source.

Under the direction of the KGB, Vincenzo distanced himself from Slipyj and Fedoruk. At a press conference in Lviv, Vincenzo denounced Slipyj and other clergymen, saying that "under the concealment of religion they have engaged in political activities against the USSR, incompatible with their duties as priests."

For his valuable services, Vincenzo was released from criminal responsibility for his currency violation, on the recommendation of the KGB.

A number of beneficial factors have emerged which have allowed us to cause considerable damage to religious sects, preventing the creation of new religious groups and creating internal leadership rivalries in religious institutions, by exploiting their careerism, greed, and moral disillusionment.

---

41. The OUN continued underground armed resistance to Soviet rule into the late 1950s, and it was also active abroad in coordinating anticommunist activities with other émigré groups from Eastern Europe (except for those from Poland), and eventually with those from Cuba and southeast Asia. The OUN was covertly supported by the Vatican, the CIA, and MI6. Bishop Yosadat Fedoruk spent much of his life between 1946 and 1960 in Soviet prisons for his support of the banned Ukrainian Greek Catholic Church. During his time in exile from 1960 to 1967 Slipyj appointed him the clandestine bishop for Greek Catholics in Soviet Central Asia, a post he secretly resumed in Frunze (now named Bishkek), the capital of the Kyrgyz Soviet Socialist Republic. He died on December 21, 1979.

Before his expulsion from the USSR in 1963, Slipyj decided on Vasyl Velychovsky as his successor to lead the Uniate spiritual community. Velychovsky shared Slipyj's hostile attitude towards the Soviet authorities. Having knowledge of the unpleasant relationship between Velychovsky and some Uniate clergy and monks, both the KGB of the USSR and the KGB in the Lviv region moved to morally compromise Velychovsky in the minds of the members of the Basilian Monastery, of the students, and of the White clergy. In these operations, the KGB made extensive use of the agents "Tikhov," "Sidorenko," "Romanenko," "Sova," and "Podolenin," who worked to create this negative opinion of Velychovsky. When Slipyj dispatched his emissaries to the Ukraine, we made use of our agent "Tikhov" to verify their identities and activities. These actions allowed us to break the unity of the Uniate believers, dividing them into supporters of Velychovsky and those groups that are opposed to him. These tactics led to isolation of the Uniate clergy in the Zakarpatska Region, who, under the influence of our agents, rejected the efforts of Velychovsky to be recognized as their leader, although later he was able to get his subordinate Sterniuk appointed to the Galicia Archdiocese.[42] The clergy refused to recognize the leadership of Velychovsky and Sterniuk, who in the past had served the Stanislavsky and Peremishlensky Dioceses. Through the efforts of agent "Natasha," believers were provided with widespread evidence of Sterniuk's violations of his monastic codes. Our agents also provided this evidence to the Vatican, with the result that he lost a considerable amount of support among the Uniates.[43]

Chairman of the KGB Yuri Andropov approved, on April 4, 1969, the following measures by the KGB to strengthen the fight against subversion by the Vatican and the Uniates to be implemented over a two year period from 1969 to 1970.[44]

---

42. Vlodomyr Sterniuk (1907–1997), a Redemptorist, served a sentence of five years of hard labor in a Soviet prison camp.

43. Despite the KGB's optimism that Velychovsky was thoroughly compromised in Slipyj's eyes, there is little historical evidence to support this conclusion, as both Mitrokhin and Christopher Andrew have noted in their work *The Sword and the Shield: The Mitrokhin Archive and the Secret History of the KGB*.

44. For much of the Brezhnev period, Yuri Andropov (KGB chairman 1967–1982) was, along with ideology boss Mikhail Suslov, the *eminence grise* of the Soviet Politburo, much like Konstantin Pobedonostsev, the Ober-Procurator of the Holy Synod, was during the reigns of Alexander III and Nicholas II in the Tsarist Empire. Andropov had

1. Gain influence over a few members of the Roman Curia (Bishops Katkov, Maie, Gromilon, and others), and invite them to the Soviet Union, where we can implement measures to gain information about the Vatican and its leaders.

Executors of this operation included the Fifth Department of the KGB, and the KGB in Lithuania, Latvia, Byelorussia, Ukraine, and Moscow.

2. Make use of KGB agents in the Congregation on the Question of Eastern Churches, the Secretariat on Religious Affairs and Atheism, the Secretariat on Christian Unity, the Collegium Russicum, the Pontifical College of Saint Casimir, the Ukrainian Pontifical College of Saint Josaphat, and the Ecumenical Center in Finland, all of these organizations prepare cadres for work in the USSR.

Existing operations have used agents "Rass," "Apostol," and "Sluga," having made use of their contacts within the USSR.

3. Undertake combined measures to compromise and discredit clerical émigrés, and to deepen the conflict among its leaders Archbishop Buchko, Bishops Bryzgys and Sloskans,[45] Prelates Tulab, Ignatavichus, Vaishnor, and others, who support close ties with nationalist organizations.

---

been Soviet ambassador to Budapest during the Hungarian Revolution in 1956, and the event convinced him that only constant surveillance and control—and, if necessary, overwhelming force—could keep the populations under Communist rule in line. Andropov was clearly the number two figure in the Soviet regime from the late 1960s to the early 1980s, and succeeded Brezhnev as General Secretary of the Communist Party of the Soviet Union.

45. On May 19, 1943, the Jewish Telegraphic Agency reported that, according to a communication from the Polish government in exile, Bishop Vincentas Bryzgys (1903–1992) "has excommunicated all Lithuanians participating in or assisting Nazis in the persecution of Jews and Poles." In sharp contrast, the Nuremberg War Crimes Trial Archives at Columbia University have documents that outline his collaboration with the Nazis. See Rochelle Saidel, *The Outraged Conscience: Seekers of Justice for Nazi War Criminals in America* (Albany, New York: SUNY Press, 1984), pp. 61, 62. Bishop Boleslavs Sloskans (1893–1981) was the Latvian-born Bishop of Minsk who spent nearly all of 1927 to 1933 in Soviet prisons on false charges of espionage; he returned to Latvia in 1933 and then Belgium in 1944, and spent much of the rest of his life as the *in absentia* leader of Catholics in the Sovet Republics in Estonia, Latvia, and Byelorussia.

4. The goal is to compel the Vatican to suspend its subversive activities towards the Soviet republics of the Baltic States, the Ukraine, and Byelorussia, by providing disinformation to Pope Paul VI, claiming that actions hostile to the Soviet regime, provoked by foreign Catholic centers, have occurred in our territory. Also, to support the creation of Catholic centers in these Soviet republics, independent of the Vatican.[46]

5. This disinformation was provided to the Vatican by agent "Adamant," making use of contacts with prominent members of the Roman Curia, as well as agent "Daktaras" who, in October, traveled to Rome with a large group of bishops and had a personal meeting with the pope.

The PGU, also known as the Fifth Department of the KGB, and the KGB in the Lithuanian SSR were active in these assignments; they were also able to place agent "Uralskogo" in the Jesuit order.

6. In October 1969, in the city of New York, consultations were held on the issue of the arms race and the struggle for peace, convened by American Catholic organizations. Among the staff of the Soviet delegation involved in these meetings were agents "Adamant," "Kuznetsov," "Zelenogorskogo," and other operatives. They also worked to disrupt the efforts of those among the Americans who wanted to use these forums for anti-Soviet objectives.

7. At the request of Secret Police organs in the GDR (East Germany), we developed an operation involving the Catholic Bishop Schaffran, using an agent residing in the GDR, a KGB agent named "Zhigimantas."[47] This agent was able to win the trust of Schaffran, which allowed for meetings with the pope. "Zhigimantas" was invited by Schaffran to an introductory

---

46. The idea that, if religious institutions could not be eradicated under Socialism, they could and should be isolated from their fellow churches beyond the Iron Curtain, was not limited to the Soviet government in its handling of the Eastern Rite Catholic churches and the Vatican. The East German regime pursued a similar idea with regards to the *Evangelische Kirche* in the GDR, pressuring it in the late 1960s to cut ties with its sister Protestant communities in West Germany.

47. Gerhard Schaffran served as Auxiliary Bishop of Gorlitz from 1962 to 1970, and in 1970 became bishop of the Catholic Diocese of Meissen (in 1979 renamed the Diocese of Dresden-Meissen), where he served until 1987. One of the most prominent Catholic clergymen in the history of the GDR, Schaffran supervised the only assembly of high-ranking Catholic clergy in East Germany, in July 1987, shortly before his retirement.

meeting with the Priests Marowitz and Frimel, who arrived from Lithuania in 1969.

8. The Fifth Department of the KGB, along with Chekist (secret police) organs in Hungary, conducted an operation to cultivate the Uniate Bishop Dudash, who was residing in the Hungarian People's Republic; he was a member of the Vatican's Congregation of the Eastern Churches. This operation involved an agent of the KGB code-named "Potochin," who had been in Hungary for a brief amount of time. The agent was able to meet with Dudash and gain his trust.[48]

9. The KGB placed agents in several Vatican organizations, drawing from influential figures who had engaged in previous operations within the Russian Orthodox Church ("Drozdov," "Sviatoslav," "Adamant," and "Nesterov"). Their task was to infiltrate different Vatican organizations: the Congregation for the Eastern Churches, the Secretariat for the Unity of Christians, and the Secretariat for Justice and Peace, all of which prioritize the establishment of closer relations with the Russian Orthodox Church, these organizations hoped with their assistance to enter into contact with government agencies.

10. In 1968, the KGB received evidence of a plan by the Secretariat of State of the Vatican to use religious language and political appeals to undermine the USSR. The leaders selected for this assignment were chosen from the staff of the deputy secretary of state, Cardinal Benelli. In anticipation of these attempts by the Vatican, the Soviet press published news articles to expose this plan.

There are several successful examples of recruitment of informers from the Uniate communities. One of the Uniate leaders, codenamed "Serafim" in the past, was head of a monastery and a Doctor of Theology. Before his recruitment, he had been arrested twice and prosecuted for active participation in anti-Soviet activities; had established extensive connections with Uniate clergy; and had achieved a broad popularity with believers. The first attempt to make contact with Serafim occurred in 1964, soon after he was released from prison. At this meeting with a KGB operative, Serafim acted

---

48. Outside of the Ukrainian SSR, Hungary, Romania, Czechoslovakia and Poland also had small Eastern Rite religious communities. The Romanian contingent also suffered harsh persecution following the Second World War.

insincerely, and tried to avoid any further meetings. He then traveled to Siberia, where he engaged in missionary work among Catholics. This long work with parts of the population hostile to the Soviet government helped to overcome his reluctance to working with us.

Then Serafim returned to the Lviv Region, desiring to register to live in one of the central districts. We decided to take advantage of it. An "accidental" meeting was organized there with a well-known operative. Serafim met with this operative, an old acquaintance, informing the acquaintance of his positive relationship with the Soviet authorities and his intention to remain in the Lviv Region. This allowed for continued contacts with the Chekist, who cultivated Serafim as a potential informant. At the initial meeting, the Chekist spoke at length with Serafim about the hostile, anti-Soviet essence of the Uniate Church. Serafim was shown the Uniate anti-Soviet journals "Missionary" and "Niva," clippings from the dispatches of an envoy from the head of the Uniate Church Sheptytsky, and photo documents revealing the involvement of Greek Catholic clergy with the SS Divisions in Galicia and with the bandit forces of Stepan Bandera in their fight against the Soviet government.[49] The agent quoted selections from anti-Soviet statements by Bishops Buchko and Korneliak, and provided anti-Soviet nationalist articles from the Munich newspaper *Christian Voice*.

The recruitment of Serafim occurred at one of these meetings. The proposal of secret cooperation with the KGB was agreed to without hesitation; it appeared as if he had already prepared for this possibility. On the written agreement, Serafim used his personal pseudonym "Volynskiy" for his signature. At this meeting, he informed us of hostile activities of Archbishop Velychovsky and Bishop Eksuhan, who had appointed two more bishops and abbots of domestic Uniate orders, and he told us about illegal courses for the training of youths as monks. The proposal of cooperation did contain one

---

49. Stepan Bandera was the leader of the Organization of Ukrainian Nationalists (*Orhanizatsiya Ukrayins'kykh Natsionalistiv*, or OUN) during the Second World War, who fought both the Soviet and the Nazi regimes to create an independent Ukrainian state. Escaping to West Germany at the end of the war, he continued to direct efforts by the remnants of the Ukrainian Insurgent Army against the Soviet regime until his assassination by an agent of the KGB in Munich in 1959. The Soviets spent much of the forty years following the Second World War waging a propaganda war against Bandera and his cause. He remains a controversial figure to this day in Ukraine and Russia.

statement that was rejected very painfully, but the Chekist did not insist on his agreement with it. For religious people, a signed statement of collaboration is a severe psychological ordeal, causing considerable fear of God's lengthy punishment in the next world. It is well known that, having signed a statement of cooperation, an operative may then, on bended knee, try to persuade the KGB agent to return it, expressing their fear of "going to Hell."

Serafim's psychological transformation supported the KGB's use of active measures during this time, which included exposing the hostile actions of the underground Uniate Church and the arrest of their leader Velychovsky. KGB observers noticed that Serafim was quite ambitious, and desired to surpass other Uniate authorities in importance. Playing on these feelings, our KGB agents used this knowledge to gain his trust, and to receive from him confidential information about the Uniate underground organizations. Serafim described in detail how illegal instructions were given to the Uniate monks, when they were given, and by whom. He told us about criminal activities of the organization of Velychovsky, the Bishop's personal connections in the Soviet Union and abroad and the hierarchical structure of the monks and their leadership, which necessitated the provision of lists of illegal Uniate clergy. Serafim's answers were tape-recorded.

In the process of documenting the illegal Uniate activities of the abbot of Vasiliansky Monastery Elen Manko, specifically religious gatherings he led, we devoted attention to the nun Anastasia, a nurse from the Lviv Polyclinical Institute.[50] Through the efforts of agent "Skrando" (a former monk from the Basilian Order), it was established that Anastasia had the full trust of Manko and made use of it. Manko purchased in Lviv a private house for the monks, which was placed in the name of Anastasia. Anastasia was characterized as a cunning, self-interested woman, sometimes violating her monastic vows, engaging in drinking with close friends, going to the movies, and avoiding her work as a nurse. According to information pro-

---

50. "The Basilian Order" referred to in the document is the Congregation of Saint Basil the Great, originally formed in Vilnius in 1631. It was among the most active of the Greek Catholic orders in both Lithuania and the Ukraine until its suppression by the Soviet government and absorption by the Russian Orthodox Church after WWII. It continued its clandestine activities for the next forty years, and publicly resumed its work in the Ukraine after the fall of the USSR. The Vasiliansky Monastery still exists in the suburbs of Lviv.

vided by agent "Zoi," Anastasia intended to pass herself off in correspondence as the owner of the property; due to her hostile feelings towards Manko, this information was concealed from her associates.

Her detention for assisting the illegal meetings of the monks, as well as the detention of her own sister, strongly transformed Anastasia, creating great concern for her own and her sister's welfare. Investigation revealed that when she was a child, Anastasia was educated at the Vasiliansky Monastery; Manko had served as their primary instructor. During the war, he supported the Ukrainian Nationalist insurgents and allowed one of them to live at the monastery. Anastasia's brother, in 1944, willingly volunteered to serve in an SS Division in Galicia and was later killed in combat.[51] She attempted to find his letters in the archives, which were written from Germany to the Archdeacon Kliment Sheptytsky, the brother of the Metropolitan. The author of the letter swore allegiance to the fascist regime and to Hitler personally. All of these materials were utilized with the goal of converting Anastasia to work for us. Shortly afterwards, contact was made with Anastasia. When she was offered the opportunity to work with the KGB, she agreed in writing, and received the code name "Polina." This collaboration was treated seriously, with her providing a considerable number of useful materials.

For the cultivation of leading Uniates, the KGB used one of the leaders of the monastic order, Abrosim, who lived in Lviv. His contacts with and support of the Uniates were punished with exile to a special settlement. Upon his return to Lviv, he reestablished connections with Uniates and engaged in a number of secret trips abroad in order to meet with Catholic authorities: Cardinal Wyszyński, Bishop Tokarchuk, General Vicar Grinnik of the Uniate Church in the Polish People's Republic, the archdeacon of the monastic students in the Vatican "Chornim" (Black), and others. Agents "Skidnji" and "Pravdivji" characterized Abrosim as a cunning person, "shrewd," inclined to decide all questions quietly, without fuss, able to find

---

51. Despite the horrendously cruel occupation policies of the Nazis in the *Reichskommissariat Ukraine* and *Reichskommissariat Ostland*, over 1,000,000 Soviet citizens collaborated in some capacity with the Germans during the Nazi-Soviet war from 1941–1945, according to Aleksandr Solzhenitsyn. The real number was almost certainly much higher than that.

a common language and to be on good terms with various different office holders. In his conspiratorial efforts, Abrosim often collaborated with his sister Maria.

Acquiring an agent who was one of the veterans of the Uniate leadership was a crucial lynchpin. The KGB made many attempts to achieve this. Abrosim announced that he had never attempted to conceal his illegal activities among the Uniates. His factual evidence proved this, as he provided evidence of illegal activities, which could then be deciphered by our agents. The key to establishing personal contact with our emerging recruit was, in the case of Abrosim, our threats to kill his sister Maria. This led him to provide valuable answers to the KGB's many questions regarding Uniate activities.

Through the efforts of our agents and other operative activities, certain details were revealed about the life, actions, and characteristics of Maria and other relatives of Abrosim. Maria's husband was ill with schizophrenia, which gave him delusions of persecution, often beating her because of his jealousy. The daughter of Maria, Miroslava, had years ago left a marriage to a man who developed mental retardation. Abroism had never approved of this marriage. He was entirely dedicated his family, with a close understanding of their desires, demonstrating his love for family members, he provided them with material assistance, looking after the needs of Maria's children, providing them with gifts. This information convinced the KGB that they had enough evidence regarding Maria's life and her connections to Abrosim.

The formal recruitment efforts began with the fact that Abrosim was summoned by the OVIR (Office of Visa and Registration) upon his exit from Poland in connection with his efforts in that country. The OVIR then turned Abrosim over to the KGB. Disparaging him without leaving out any details, Abrosim was presented with evidence concerning his activities on behalf of the Uniate Church, information about his sister's personal life, and further material provided by our operative workers derived from Maria's family. The "monk" lost the gift of speech; he was staggered, and at a total loss. His wandering eyes, shaking hands, perspiration, and frequent covering of his face, all revealed intense mental suffering. The KGB took note of some obvious facts to conceive of this trap. Considering it useless to avoid confessing to his guilt, Abrosim told us about the apparatus of the illegal leadership of the (Uniate) monastic orders in the Ukraine, naming many authorities and monks, including those who had arrived in Lviv under the guise of tourism, and about his 1971 visit to Poland and his meetings with these individuals. About a month after this meeting, Abrosim was recruited under the self-selected code name "Irinei," the document of which he refused to sign. The written record of the recruitment meeting provided sufficient assurance.

"Irinei" came to believe in his sister's collaboration with the KGB, often putting forward the conversational phrase, "Surely, you already got this information from my sister Maria."[52]

Beginning shortly after his recruitment, "Irinei" expressed continuing surprise that his late sister kept her secret connections with the KGB from him.

In 1981, the Politburo of the Communist Party in the Ukraine addressed the subject "Concerning Successful Measures to Prevent the Activities of the Catholic Church and the revival of Uniates in the Ukraine." They produced an article in newspapers and a program segment on radio stations entitled "The Uniate Church—An Enemy to Peace and Progress."

5.

Hungarian Chekists developed a proposal from the State Committee for Religious Affairs, to prompt the Hungarian clerical delegation to the Vselensky Assembly to put forward a proposal to recognize the episcopal body of Hungary as the unified representative of the Hungarian Church and clergy residing abroad. Their agents circulated the idea that the Hungarian clergy in the country were annoyed that the Vatican continued to recognize exile priests Zagon and Mester as go-betweens of the Vatican and Hungary. This idea emerged from evidence that was taken from the Vatican files by their agents. Joseph Zagon was a prelate, a citizen of Austria, and the director of the Hungarian Pontifical Institute in Rome. He was also a leader of Hungarian emigres. Mester was also a priest and served as the deputy director of the Hungarian Papal Institute. Komornik was the Director of the

---

52. Recruiting informants by telling them that family members and/or friends had already informed on them was a common tactic by secret police forces throughout the Soviet bloc.

Administration in the Hungarian Ministry of Internal Affairs who dealt with these two clergy.[53]

Once, at the beginning of the second session of the Vselensky Assembly, Zagon presented disinformation concerning the position of the Church in Hungary, clearly serving the Vatican's reactionary interests. Zagon's insulting tone had wounded the leadership of the Hungarian Church; however, its delegation was easily able to refute his claims. All it achieved was to create further estrangement between Zagon and his Hungarian colleagues. Regarding actual events in religious life in Hungary, the Vatican deluded itself, thinking that these priests could provide them with objective information and could provide a connection between the Vatican and the Hungarian Church.

The Hungarian Chekists introduced channels in the Vselensky Assembly for the distribution of letters and the creation of publications, to turn Hungarian émigrés against the Hungarian Pontifical Institute and against its director Zagon. The Chekists had foreseen that the Vatican would condemn modernistic currents as weakening the foundations of the Church.[54]

In the Hungarian People's Republic, 63% of the population is Catholic, 82% baptize their children in Catholic churches, 55% are married in the Church, and 81% are buried in Church cemeteries. The Catholic Church in Hungary has about 4,000 employees as of 1967.

From July 24 to 27, 1967, a conference of Chekists was held in Budapest, with representatives from the USSR, Bulgaria, Hungary, the GDR, Poland, Czechoslovakia, and Romania. Many leaders of the political police in these countries attended, as did their deputies. Among the central issues discussed were actions against the Vatican, measures to compromise the Vatican and

---

53. Mitrokhin refers to Komornik, without giving him a first name or even initial, as a Director of Administration V of the Hungarian MVD. This is probably as a mistake on the part of Mitrokhin, as Komornik probably worked for Department III/3-1-A, which was dedicated to combating the influence of the Roman Catholic Church

54. Until the deal that allowed Cardinal József Mindszenty to leave the American embassy in Budapest and go into exile in the West, the Hungarian Catholic Church's leadership structure was effectively frozen in place, which made any attempts by the leadership of the Hungarian Catholic Church, as well as the Vatican, to make an accommodation with János Kádár's regime very difficult, although some minor concessions were made on both sides in 1964.

its followers, bringing about internal divisions within the Vatican, and also divisions between the Vatican and numerous capitalist countries. The KGB of the USSR was represented by Agaiants, Khamazyuk, and Kulikov. At the conference, Agaiants and Khamazyuk spoke on the theme "Concerning the hostile activities of the Vatican, Catholic and Uniate clergy in the territory of the USSR and attempts by the security organs to act against these activities." Kulikov spoke on the theme "Some questions regarding Agent-Operative work within the institutions of the Vatican."

Andropov stressed that the meeting supported the proposal of the KGB on the desirability of working against the Vatican in close connection with work against the main enemy, the United States. The actions of the Romanian delegation at the conference were also noted, as they did not sign off on the protocol of the meeting.

"Gobbs"—Khalash Lajos, 6.7.1927, born in the village of Yedied, Hungary, an ethnic Hungarian, but a citizen of Austria. Agent of the Hungarian Organs of State Security. He was recruited in 1962 in Hungary, after attempting to take religious pictures that were to be transferred to the Hungarian Church Administration. "Gobbs" a priest-missionary, became a member of a missionary order, the Societias Verbi Divini (SVD, the Society of the Divine Word) in Austria. Following his completion of the Insitutuion of Higher Learning of the Order of SVD of Saint Gabriel in 1951, "Gobbs" traveled to the Philippines to serve as a monk-missionary. His mother and brother remained in Austria.

With Gobbs' release in 1967, a condition of his parole was connected to this question:

"Do you know the Abbey of Pannonhalma in Hungary?"
Answer: "I do not, but I know the abbot, Abbot Zire."

In 1974, he was expelled from the network of agents, as the Hungarians could not possibly support his mission in the Philippines and were not interested in it. "Gobbs" during this time resided on the island of Mindoro.

The KGB was interested in working with "Gobbs" and desired to establish an agent relationship. They made contact with him in 1979, and in 1980–1981.

The Hungarian authorities wrote "Gobbs" a letter, but never received an answer.

Upon his return to Europe, "Gobbs" offered his support and connections to Hungarian agents. "Gobbs" promised to hide any person in the building of the Spiritual Mission, in the event of a War.

6.

At a meeting on July 17, 1967, the Central Committee agreed on the creation of a department of the KGB designed to fight ideological diversions. In 1968, order #0051 was published for the KGB, "Concerning the task of the Organs of State Security in the fight against Ideological Diversions created by our opponents." The report acknowledged that fighting ideological diversions is one of the most important tasks ahead of the KGB, linked to the class struggle, the fight for the Soviet man and for his livelihood and freedom, and to strengthen the position of socialism and communism. Work against these opponents assumed an aggressive character, with a clear awareness of the reactionary plans of foreign ideological centers and organizations. The task before us was to place KGB agents in these institutions, and to obtain valuable information, and for the VGU and the Fifth Department of the KGB to strengthen the fight against ideological diversions in these countries.[55]

The KGB distributed the directive "Concerning the Hostile Activities of the Vatican against socialist countries and the worldwide Communist movement." The directive was distributed to 24 KGB residents across the world to inform their assigned tasks.

The KGB resident in Rome noted the difficulty of infiltrating the Vatican. Over a thousand people work there, among them exists considerable mistrust, new faces and people are quickly recognized, and the Vatican strictly reports all contact between workers and inhabitants in the Vatican and all Soviet citizens.

"Tantsor" (Hungarian for "Dancer") (aka "Verdi"), Rossi Frederico, born in 1909, grew up in Rome, an Italian citizen, a religious believer, but

---

55. "VGU" is an acronym for *Vtoroy Glavnoye Upravlenniie*, the Second Chief Directorate of the KGB, which was in charge of all internal security matters—those within Soviet borders.

an opponent of the Vatican, worked as the vice-secretary of the Universal Labor Conference. He was a former member of the Christian Democratic Party. After leaving the Christian Democrats, he attempted to join the Italian Communist Party. Di Vittorio, general secretary of the Universal Labor Federation, informed him that for the good of the Communists, if in his heart Frederico wanted to join them, he could assist them by continuing to work with the Christian Democrats.

Di Vittorio told Frederico, "It is not important if you have a Communist Party membership card or not; what is important is that you are willing to work for the Communist Party."[56]

Frederico believed that many Catholic clergy used the Church to pursue politically reactionary goals, in the interest of capitalism; on the other hand, he considered Protestants to be of a higher quality, but they too were not true Marxist-Leninists. Although he did not support either one, a visit to Tashkent in November 1950 convinced him that Marxism-Leninism was the science above all sciences.

Upon his return to Italy from the Soviet Union in 1950, he was assigned a task at the Vatican—penetrating American organizations in Italy. "Tantsor" reported that the open fight with the Vatican had not achieved positive results. It would be better to create groups of priests, carefully persuade them with antigovernment propaganda, and disseminate democratic ideas among them, all the while maintaining their ranks and identities as priests. Other priests who openly supported Soviet goals quickly lost their prestige, being stripped of their clerical titles. For example, Don Gadzero had joined with the supporters of peace, but was then removed from his duties as a priest. Tondi, who was a professor at the Gregorian University, spoke out directly against the Vatican, which did have a political effect, but he was subsequently removed from his parish, losing his connections to other Catholic believers.[57] Don Spadon, in Bologna, preached theological lessons

---

56. In other sections of his archive, Mitrokhin revealed the identities of a number of KGB agents who worked as "illegals" in both Christian and Social Democratic parties in Western Europe.

57. Alighiero Tondi (1908–1979), a Jesuit, who left the order and joined the Italian Communist party, for which he was excommunicated. He spied for the Soviet Union.

resembling Protestantism, advocating a personal relationship with God. Because of this, was required to leave the Church.

"Tantsor" established a relationship with an agent at the KGB Resident office in Rome, Mamochin. In 1952, this was transformed into a confidential connection, as "Tantsor" was well-informed about a broad range of social activities and himself proposed a number of informational possibilities.

In 1968, the KGB brought three agents to Rome: "Roshchin," "Petrov," and "Antanas." In April 1968, the KGB Resident in Rome embarked on work directed against the Vatican, using a head operative named Youzenas, from the KGB of the Lithuanian SSR.

"Zhibut," an agent of the Lithuanian KGB, was a priest who worked from May 21 to June 11 of 1969 in Rome, on the Working Commission for the Reform of the Canon Law Codex.

"Vladimir" was a part of a delegation of the Russian Orthodox Church who took part in the Second Vatican Council.

"Antanas" was a KGB agent, a citizen of the USSR, and a Lithuanian. Currently engaged in study in Rome, he arrived in Rome from the USSR on January 17, 1968.

"Petrov" was an agent of the KGB, and a citizen of the USSR of Slavic nationality. Currently engaged in study in Rome, he arrived on January 17, 1968.

"Missionary," real name Katkov Andrei, was a Russian, specialist in the Vatican for Russian affairs. He was recruited for work in the KGB through the efforts of agent "Roshchin."[58]

Arranz Miguel, born in 1930, raised in Guadalajara, Spain, is a Basque. He is vice-rector of the Collegium Russicum, a professor of Liturgy, a

---

His story is told in Matteo Manferdini's *Il Gesuita Comunista: Vita estrema di Alighiero Tondi, spia in vaticano* (Soveria Mannelli: Rubbettino Editore, 2020).
    58. Andrei Katkov, MIC (1916–1995), was titular bishop of Nauplia and attended the Second Vatican Council.

member of the Jesuits, and active in Rome. He began a residency in Rome in 1969.[59]

"Ost" is a notable journalist, who in the past was a parliamentary deputy from a Monarchist party. He is also an agent working for the KGB Resident in Rome. "Ost" has gotten closer with colleagues working in the Vatican, having received information from the most powerful Jesuits in Italy concerning conversations between Paul VI and Richard Nixon in 1969.

Activities of the KGB in 1968-1969 in its efforts against the Vatican: The KGB turned to compromising the Vatican by exposing its various reactionary activities; to sow and strengthen divisions and discontentment; to organize dossiers of official and agent material concerning the criminal activities of Archbishop Mykola Bychok, Bishop Bryzgys, Sloskans, and prelates Tulab, Ignatavich, and Vaicius, and to create schisms between the Vatican and religious institutions such as the Worldwide Council of Churches, the Worldwide Council of Lutherans and the Worldwide Council of Baptists.[60]

KGB Residents might exploit the Antioch, Alexandrian, Coptic, and Armenian Churches, and the Ukrainian Autocephalous Church in Canada, gaining influence over the leaders of these Churches, to push them to make public proclamations against the influence of the Vatican over these organizations.

Active measures on the part of the KGB: In Paris, it published a brochure entitled "What did you do with the legacy of Pope John XXIII?" The brochure exposed the right-wing course of the new leadership of the Catholic Church.

For secret police organs in Hungary, the KGB prepared a brochure that exposed the part played by clergy of different religious sects in the countries

---

59. When the Metropolitan of the Russian Orthodox church met with Pope John Paul I on September 5, 1978, the Metropolitan suffered a heart attack, from which he died. Arranz was the official translator that day, which occurred just three weeks before the passing of Pope John Paul I.

60. The entrance of the Russian Orthodox Church into the World Council of Churches was considered by the KGB and the Council of Religious Affairs as a coup for their diplomacy, as they would use their influence in the WCC to support Soviet foreign policy goals.

of Latin America, in the fight against American expansionism and in support of National Liberation Movements, emphasizing the refusal of the Catholic Church to support them in these efforts. This brochure, published in 1969, was made possible through the efforts of Hungarian intelligence agents in Latin America.

"Uniat" is the codename of Johann Krammer, born in 1944, raised in the town of Saint Polten, Austria. He is an Austrian citizen who has a master's degree in theology. Connection with him was established by the KGB in 1969. He provided information about the activities of the Uniate Church, about Cardinal Slipyj, Uniates, and the Vatican. Slipyj is the head of the Uniate Catholic Center.

The Actions of "Uniat" were undertaken on behalf of the Exarchate of the Ukrainian Russian Orthodox Church.[61]

"Roglin" and "Petrov" are agents of the Fifth Department of the KGB. They were trained in the Collegium Russicum. They left for study in 1968 and both returned to Moscow after completing their studies in 1970.

In 1969, "Roglin" and "Petrov" were in Belgium and France and became acquainted with the activities of the Catholic centers.

From May 11 to 15, 1970, in Budapest, a meeting occurred between the Chekist organs of the USSR and Hungary, focused on work against the Vatican. Among those who took part were the Head of the Fifth Department of the PGU of the KGB, Colonel A. I. Kulikov; Assistant Head of the Fifth Department of the PGU, L. P. Morozov; the Hungarian Vice-Head of the Vatican Department, Földes; and his Deputy Director Bereni. Both sides raised questions and expressed opinions about Vatican politics and its new directions that had emerged in 1968; the internal strength of the Vatican; its relationship with various socialist countries; negotiations between the Vatican and the Hungarian authorities; work against the Vatican in a number of countries, including Italy, France, Austria, and Belgium; the methods of plac-

---

61. This once again testifies to the dark partnership between the Russian Orthodox Church and the Soviet government in the Ukrainian SSR, at least when it came to acting against the Ukrainian Greek Catholic Church continuing from the late 1940s into the late 1960s.

ing agents among the churches; joint activities against the Vatican; and exchange of information. Földes emphasized that work against the Vatican was one of the main tasks of Hungarian intelligence.[62] Because of the importance and scale of this task, over 30 operatives are engaged in it. It occupied two different sections of the Hungarian intelligence organs. The main focus of the Rome resident of Hungarian intelligence were efforts against the Vatican, while the residents in Vienna and Paris also have special agents engaged in undercover work in the Church. The ability to recruit new sources has improved the quality of information; however, they have not been able to penetrate the Vatican itself and are reliant on documentary evidence.

The Soviet Chekists also met with the Head of the European Department of Intelligence for Hungary, Radnale, discussing work against NATO and its activities.

In April 1971, the Center received a message from the KGB Resident in Rome that it would be premature to make a direct connection between a Vatican proposal to internationalize all holy sites in Jerusalem and the initiative of the Soviet government at the United Nations Security Council to transfer all Israeli lands to Arab countries.

Andropov informed the Central Committee of the CPSU on May 14, 1971 that the KGB received a particularly important document from our Polish friends, a stenographic written record of a meeting between Tito and Pope Paul VI during the visit of the Yugoslavian leader to Italy on March 29, 1971.

In a letter, Andropov wrote:

We should direct our attention to Tito's frank remarks concerning the position of the Yugoslav government towards the crisis in the Middle East. Tito emphasized that Cairo is "fully Russian" and "it is difficult to say what they will decide." Regarding the question of the convening of a pan-European conference, Tito declared that Yugoslavia expressed a desire to

---

62. Despite the status of Cardinal Mindszenty serving as a stumbling block, the Hungarian government and the Vatican had reached a series of limited accommodations from the mid-1960s to the early 1970s, especially regarding the appointment of bishops. Both John XXIII and Paul VI were eager to have some dialogue with Communist regimes during this period, as part of *Ostpolitik*. If nothing else, the Vatican wished to keep the ecclesiastical hierarchy in place on the eastern side of the Iron Curtain.

"prepare for an excellent meeting." However, he noted, until this happened "It would continue to provide dialogue between the two blocs."[63]

"Monach" is Miguel Arrantz, a Jesuit, and a professor at the Pontifical Oriental Institute in Rome. He studied at the Leningrad Spiritual Academy and wrote a dissertation to receive a Master's Degree in Theology. In 1975, he taught a lecture course at the Leningrad Spiritual Academy.

The KGB Resident in Rome, on the information provided by the agent "Jesuit," recommended sending an invitation from the Soviet Union to the Jesuit Superior General Arrupe, in order to put him in a beneficial mood towards the USSR. Arrupe appears to be a confidant of Pope Paul VI.

In June 1971, Patriarch Pimen I of Moscow and all of Russia contacted Superior General Arrupe, inviting him to the USSR. The KGB planned to use this opportunity to approach a number of members of his order for service in the KGB.

"Professor," an agent of the KGB, was in Rome from September 7 to 21, 1973 by invitation, for the consecration of Cardinal Felicia. In the Vatican, he met with Cardinal Slipyj. In order to strengthen his position, the KGB proposed to "Professor" that he organize a meeting with the Uniate leadership in Lviv, with Slipyj's blessing. The impetus for this meeting appeared to be a letter sent to Kurchab with information concerning the September meeting of the General Assembly of the Uniates and a new election to replace its former procurator, Pfab. The letter was transmitted through illegal channels by the Parisian Greek Catholic Priest Levints, a Ukrainian by nationality.

In 1974, the KGB Resident in Rome presented before its agents the following penetration tasks regarding the Vatican:

With regards to the Secretariat of State of the Vatican, it is necessary to answer questions regarding the direction of its foreign policy, by acquiring documents regarding the activities of the Vatican in both capitalist and socialist countries.

---

63. Yugoslavia, although a Communist dictatorship, had been independent from Moscow since the Tito-Stalin split in 1947, and, along with Egypt and India, was a leader of the "non-aligned movement" during its heyday from the mid-1950s to the early 1970s.

One section of agents will be engaged in obtaining intelligence regarding the strategic line of activities by the Catholic Church in the sphere of international relations, while the other section will deal with technical questions regarding politics, the selection and distribution of diplomatic cadres, and finally, will establish connections with diplomatic staffs.

The Papal Diplomatic Academy prepares cadres for the Vatican Foreign Service.

The Congregation for the Eastern Churches is the center for the Vatican's anticommunist activities against countries of the Socialist camp. Other anticommunist operations include the Collegium Russicum, the Ukrainian Spiritual Seminary, the Pontifical Oriental Institute, the Pontifical College of Saint Casimir, and others.

The Secretariat for Non-Believers collects political information on the situation in socialist countries, and helps to develop the Vatican's political and ideological line towards the USSR and other socialist states. It is led by Cardinal Koenig.[64]

Propaganda organs of the Vatican include Vatican Radio, the newspaper *L'Osservatore Romano*, and the journal *La Civiltà Cattolica*.

KGB agents who have taken part in intelligence work regarding the Vatican include "Tourist," "Missionary," "Miloslavsky," "Albert," and "Fidelio," all of whom have trusted connections.

Agent measures regarding Vatican activities include attempts to compromise the diplomatic initiatives of the Vatican and its abilities to inspire people, to bring about divisions within the Vatican and also between the Vatican and capitalist countries, to strengthen the crisis in the Catholic Church, and to create opposition movements in the Church.

---

64. Cardinal Franz Koenig served as the Archbishop of Vienna from 1956 to 1985. Besides being active in the ecumenical movement, especially through his role in the Second Vatican Council, Koenig was one of the strongest voices for a *modus vivendi* with Communist regimes, and frequently was sent by the Vatican on diplomatic initiatives to the Soviet bloc. In 1978, he was also instrumental in securing the election of the bishop of Krakow, Karol Wojtyła, as Pope John Paul II.

The newspaper *Il Messaggero* published an article under the title "Once again with the Concordat," which criticized the prospect of a new concordat between the Vatican and the Italian government.

Shevelyov was the director of the Kerchensky Archaeological Museum during the War. After the war, he found himself abroad. He became a director of Vatican Radio. He died in 1974. It was later established that he had maintained documents in an archive, kept by his wife, Yurena Alla Shevelyov, in Rome. Andropov gave a direct order to the KGB Resident in Rome to seize control of this archive. The operation involved a number of people, including agents "Roshchin" and "Zilin." In June 1975, our agent Vladimir Stepanovich Rozhkov spent a month in Rome on the pretext of researching and preparing the defense of his dissertation about the Moscow Patriarchate. He contacted Yurena Shevelyov, who agreed to transfer the archive to the Soviet embassy, where she met Rozhkov and Shtrekov, an operative of the KGB residency.

Shevelyov's archive contained documents from the University of Munich regarding research into the Soviet Union, transcripts of broadcasts from Vatican Radio over the past ten years, documents from the archive of Prince Zhivotkov regarding the theological studies among Russian émigrés abroad in the 1930s, and other correspondence.[65]

On August 1, 1975, a KGB residency officer in Rome asked a politically and socially active Italian operative, a professor of theology named La Pierre, who has influence in the Vatican, to influence the Chilean junta through the Vatican. La Pierre, in a meeting with his operator in Florence, stated that he would fulfill this request, to exercise influence over the pope to defend Chilean Democrats in exile, including the secretary of the Chilean Communist Party, Corvalán.

The Vatican has taken steps through the Chilean Catholic Church and its diplomatic channels, with the goal of persuading the junta to liberate many political prisoners, including Luis Corvalán. Pope Paul VI made this

---

65. Vatican Radio—although not seen as quite the same threat as Radio Liberty, the Voice of America, or the BBC—was also viewed as inherently subversive, particularly with regards to broadcasts intended for Lithuania or Western Ukraine.

request through a chaplain named Chelat, who also appears to be a member of the Council for Church-State Relations.[66]

On August 15, 1975, a document written by Lieutenant General Bobkov and Lieutenant General Kryuchkov was submitted to KGB Chairman Andropov. It revealed numerous details of the Vatican's role in undermining socialism, and the measures the KGB has taken to prevent it.[67] The document outlined the activities of the Vatican on behalf of imperialism and reactionaryism, and their cooperation with the intelligence services of our enemies. The Vatican is active in sending its emissaries, in particular the Jesuits, to socialist countries. They travel in both official and illegal capacities as specialists, representatives of different firms or companies, or as tourists. They have engaged in the distribution of religious and hostile literature, and in so doing attempt to expend their influence over socialist countries. In Poland, the influence of the Catholic Church and the Vatican has strongly increased in the current period, especially since the number of open churches and trained clergy has doubled over the past two years. The Catholic Church and the Vatican also have a strong position in both Hungary and Czechoslovakia. Catholics in socialist countries use assembly in churches to activate antisocialist elements among people of various political leanings.[68]

In February 1975, in Warsaw, there was a conference of representatives of state security organs from the USSR, Bulgaria, the GDR, Hungary,

---

66. Luis Corvalán was the general secretary of the Chilean Communist Party from 1958 to 1988. Arrested on orders of General Augusto Pinochet following Pinochet's military coup on September 11, 1973, he was released in 1976 in an exchange for Soviet dissident Vladimir Bukovsky. He would spend the next twelve years in exile in the Soviet Union.

67. Vladimir Kryuchkov would take over the KGB following Andropov's elevation to General Secretary of the Communist Party in 1982. In August 1991, he would be one of the principal leaders of the State Emergency Committee, also known as the "Gang of Eight," whose failed attempt to stage a coup in Moscow to restore the pre-*glasnost* and *perestroika* order led to the rapid collapse of the Soviet Union just four months later.

68. As this report indicates, even during the era of détente in the 1970s and the papacy of Paul VI—which was certainly less hostile to the USSR than that of his predecessors—the overall "reactionary" and "threatening" character of the Vatican was never in doubt in the minds of the KGB.

Poland, Czechoslovakia, and Cuba. The Ministries of Internal Affairs of Poland, Czechoslovakia, and Hungary have placed a significant number of agents in the Vatican and in high-ranking clerical and lay Catholic circles. A plan was established to create greater coordination among these activities, using our undercover agents.

In order to identify the most valuable targets for our agents to penetrate, the First Main Directorate and the Fifth Department of the KGB, and the other special organs, planned the following:

- Obtain information about the intentions and activities of the state organs of the Vatican, especially the Secretariat of State, the Congregation for the Eastern Churches, the Secretariat for Non-Believers, and their relationship with socialist regimes.

The following individuals were specifically targeted for intelligence work: Cardinals Kazarali, Villebrand,[69] Koenig, Samore, Benelli, Podzhi, Pinedoli, and a Jesuit, John Long, an American, head of the Secretariat of State's section for relations with the Orthodox churches.

- Obtain material to give to the KGB regarding connections between the Vatican and the Fascist regimes in Italy, Germany, Spain, Portugal, and reactionary regimes in the Latin American countries and Africa, in order to compromise these connections, and introduce measures to block the Russian version of Vatican Radio.[70]
- Support the foreign policy of Pope Paul VI, specifically its more open attitude towards negotiating with socialist regimes, and provide information to the pope and his inner circle that will help elect a successor who will share this attitude. Both in public and through our agents, to support the Vatican's position for peace as well as its relations with the socialist countries—specifically, that the churches decisively come forward to promote peaceful coexistence and cooperation.

---

69. Probably Cardinal Willebrands, the Dutch cleric who headed the Society for Promoting Christian Unity.

70. The tactics of the KGB described in this section had been in use since the late Stalinist period. Pius XII was one of the most visible opponents of the Soviet regime during the early part of the Cold War.

- Undertake measures in support of progressive members of the World Council of Churches, in opposition to reactionary attempts by members of the Vatican to give an anticommunist orientation to the organization.
- Undertake measures to strengthen the position of the KGB and the special organs of our allies at the Berlin Conference of Catholics, with the goal of increasing influence over this organization and turning it against the Vatican.
- Along with our allies, introduce measures to recruit Vatican emissaries, especially those who work in the USSR, Poland, Hungary, and other countries.
- Pursue the recruitment of agents from the Institute Catholique de Paris, which collects political and economic information about the Soviet Union.[71]
- Recruit individuals from the Pontifical Academy of Theology, especially those being trained for work in the Vatican's diplomatic corps.
- Cultivate the centers of Lithuanian clerical émigrés in Rome: The Pontifical College of Saint Casimir, the Lithuanian Catholic Academy of Science, and the leading emissaries of the Lithuanian clerical émigré groups.[72]
- Cultivate the Uniate authorities: Golovatsky, leader of the Ukrainian section of Vatican Radio; Murdovo, deputy to Golovatsky; Sapeliak, the rector of St. Josaphat's Ukrainian Pontifical College in Rome, and his deputy Maziar. Obtain materials to determine whether to use these individuals in the interest of Soviet intelligence, or to compromise them.
- Determine the position of the Vatican in relation to the formation of the so-called Ukrainian Patriarchate.

---

71. Also known as the Catholic University of Paris, the school was founded in 1875, at the height of the conflict between Church and State in the French Third Republic. During the Cold War, many Catholic émigrés from the eastern side of the Iron Curtain studied there.

72. The Pontifical College of Saint Casimir was founded in Rome in 1948 by a group of Lithuanian clergy who had fled their country at the end of the Second World War. The Lithuanian Catholic Academy of Sciences was founded in Vilnius in 1922. It was abolished following the Soviet invasion in 1940, but re-founded in Rome by clerical exiles in 1956. It returned to Vilnius in 1992.

- Compromise and weaken the position of Cardinal Slipyj in the Vatican and among the Uniate authorities.[73]
- Obtain information about the summer courses in the preparation of the Uniate cadres, and the creation of a Uniate Seminary in Rome for the training of young men of Ukrainian heritage.

Nationalist impluses are on the rise in the Ukraine, Estonia, and Georgia.

Peter Nikolaus, a prelate in the West Berlin diocese, has engaged in a number of attempts to unify Catholics in the Soviet Union. The KGB will attempt to recruit him.

The Catholic Church in Poland has several clerics in the GDR, working for Polish citizens living there. In connection with this project, they have sent 14 priests to the GDR. In 1975, the organs of state security in Poland have utilized, through the Polish embassy in the GDR, an intelligence operative named Colonel Goronsky to monitor this line of activity and direct operations in response to it.

"Neptune," an agent of the KGB in the USSR, based in Kiev but fluent in the Polish language, was recruited in 1973, when he wanted to enter into the Basilian Order. The KGB prepared "Neptune" to enter into the Uniate monastery belonging to that order as an "illegal."[74]

A senior at the Rizhsky Catholic Seminary, "Viktorov" was assigned to serve as a priest in Latvia. He was not allowed to travel to other regions, but the KGB assisted him in a transfer to Ukraine, where he was then recruited.

"Lesheka," born in 1952, a Pole and a citizen of the USSR, was an agent of KGB of the USSR based in Kiev. The uncle of "Lesheka" was Alfons Zvober, born in 1921, a priest based in Poland. In 1977, "Lesheka" trained

---

73. Slipyj remained the target of KGB discrediting activities until his death on September 7, 1984. Four years later, following Gorbachev's *glasnost* and *perestroika*, the Eastern Rite churches emerged out of the shadows in the Ukrainian SSR. In August 1992, after the collapse of the Soviet Union and the emergence of an independent Ukrainian state, Slipyj's remains were interred in Saint George's Cathedral in Lviv.

74. In the terminology of the KGB, agents who worked in other countries who were not given diplomatic cover were given the designation of "illegals."

at the Pizhsky Spiritual Seminary. He planned to continue his studies in Poland, and then travel abroad. However, because he was not ordained a Priest, the Polish security services made it incredibly difficult for him to enter Poland.

Almost 800 operatives belonging to the Polish state security organs are busy at work in the Church.[75] Many of these agents are engaged in struggles against the Church. The task of these organs include the recruitment of members of Catholic organizations, gaining influence over appointments to the Catholic Church, and the selection and election of bishops.

In August 1977, the Fifth Department of the KGB in the USSR initiated a new policy with the Polish security organs, involving the transfer of Soviet citizens of Polish ancestry to engage in spiritual work in Poland.[76]

Cardinals Wyszyński and Wojtyła have established connections with workers' organizations and among the intelligentsia.

In August 1976, at the assembly of the Central Committee of the World Council of Churches, one of the questions under discussion was the violation of religious freedom by Socialist governments. The KGB and the Special Services of Cuba worked together on a line of behavior to respond to this through our agents. They successfully put forward the proposal that the task of reviewing the question of religious freedom was not one for the Central Committee, but rather one of the many points of review for the Church Commission on International Affairs, part of the Central Committee, during this period.

On June 6–10, 1977, in Moscow, a conference was held with the theme "Religious Activities for creating a secure peace, disarmament, and the improvement of relations between nations." This conference was conceived as propaganda for the peace-loving Soviet Union, and to expose Western

---

75. As events in the 1980s would show, given the size and importance of the Catholic Church in Poland, 800 operatives were not nearly enough to bring it under the control of the Polish Communist regime.

76. The vast majority of ethnic Poles who lived in the Ukrainian and Byelorussian SSRs were expelled and relocated to Poland in the first few years after 1945, although a small minority remained afterwards who could have conceivably been used by the KGB for this work.

propaganda regarding the lack of religious freedom. The conference consisted of over 500 religious believers from abroad, from all different religious faiths. The highlights of the conference were as follows:

Among the many documented events, the conference strengthened the authority of the Russian Orthodox Church in the international arena, especially in preventing the efforts of foreigners and hostile elements in the Soviet Union from using the conference to take negative action against the USSR. The conference also recognized the right of Patriarch Pimen I to declare the 2000-year celebration of the Birth of Christ. Participants at the conference continued our fight for peace. The Vatican itself was deprived of the opportunity to take initiative with regards to these decisions made at conference, which made appeals to all people of good will.

During the conference, the KGB distributed a few favorable documents regarding the positive results of the conference.

"Sportsman" Eduard Huber, born in 1922 in the village of Marktoberdorf, near Munich, is a citizen of the Federal Republic of Germany living in Rome, and a Jesuit. He is the rector of Gregorian University, and a professor of philosophy and theology. When he was in the USSR, at Moscow State University, he researched the works of Plekhanov.

"Sportsman" was recruited as a part of the Fourth Department of the Fifth Directorate of the KGB.[77] He engaged in correspondence with an agent of the Dnepropetovsk Region codenamed "Luch" and an agent of the KGB in Leningrad codenamed "Mikhailov." "Luch" is a priest, and a teacher at the school of Scientific Atheism; "Mikhailov" is also a Church worker.

In considering whether to invite "Sportsman" to the USSR and to involve the Moscow Patriarchate in attempts to recruit him, the Fifth Department of the KGB considered using him in connection with his position as a foreign resident in Rome, but arrived at the opinion about the desirability of using "Sportsman" to acquire intelligence. However, when they considered his potential value as an intelligence asset, they concluded that he had strong potential to conduct intelligence work abroad, but they

---

77. The Fourth and Fifth Departments of the Fifth Directorate of the KGB oversaw monitoring religious dissidence to the Soviet regime, both at home and abroad.

could not rule out the possibility that "Sportsman" may have connections with the special services of our opponents.

In 1978, at the home of V. Alkhimov, the Administrative Chairman of the State Bank of the USSR, a letter arrived from Amable Martinez Dias, the head of the Monastery of the Reverend Mother of God. The letter requested financial assistance, as an act of symbolism, for repairs to the monastery in connection with the 100-year anniversary of its founding. The Monastery of San Jose is in Ruiloba, in the province of Cantabria, in Spain.

In April 1979, a telegram was sent from Directorate S of the PGU to the KGB Resident in Madrid, named Resident Masolov, which informed him about the request mentioned above and provided a collection of evidence regarding the monastery and its leader, and the possibility of using him for our intentions, and in part, to provide certain documents for him. The telegram was signed by the deputy chairman of Directorate S of the PGU, Pachaevim.[78]

The Anti-Soviet Acts of John Paul II[79]

When Pope John Paul II exited the Papal Conclave in October 1978, he donated his Cardinal zucchetto to the Vilnius Archdiocese. Two members of the Archdiocese of Krakow brought the zucchetto to Vilnius to be donated to the Monastery of the Merciful Mother of God, which is in Vilnius near Aušros Vartų ("The Gates of the City").

Audrys Bačkis, a Lithuanian, was appointed by the pope to serve as the deputy head of the Vatican's Secretariat of State. Born in 1937, in the Lithuanian city of Kaunas, his father was a diplomat for "bourgeois Lithuania" in both New York and Paris. Before this appointment, Audrys Bačkis was in the Vatican diplomatic service, working on the Council for Church-State Relations.

---

78. Directorate S of the PGU (First Main Directorate) of the KGB was specifically in charge of "illegals," a Soviet term for agents working undercover in the non-communist world.

79. The perception of many observers in the West—that John Paul II's papacy was the most clearly anticommunist since that of Pius XII—was shared by many Soviet officials, including those in the KGB. This perception was sharpened by the fact that John Paul II appointed clergy from the eastern side of the Iron Curtain in key positions.

In 1979, the pope met with the dissident Moroz.[80]

The pope and the Vatican had followed a path of improving relations with China, which was welcomed from the Chinese side: there was the reopening of the Jesuit university in Shanghai, priests have been allowed to return to their work in the Church, and the Chinese press has displayed photographs of Pope John Paul II.[81]

In the Soviet press, Pope John Paul II has been accused of entering into politics, and taking positions against peace, but these accusations were presented solely as the personal opinions of those who wrote the articles, not of the Soviet government itself.

Hungarian security agencies, from their sources with unprecedented closeness to the entourage of the pope, learned in March 1980 that John Paul II had been diagnosed with spinal cancer. The illness had been concealed up to that point.[82]

On June 16, 1980, the head of KGB operations in Poland received a telegram from the Center (Moscow) detailing the following:

Our Polish friends proposed to place an important operative in a position in the Vatican, which could allow them to have unprecedented access to the pope and to the Roman congregation. In the opinion of the experi-

---

80. Valentyn Moroz (1936–2019), was sentenced to nine years in a labor camp as an "especially dangerous recidivist." On April 2, 1979, he and four other dissidents were exchanged for two Soviet spies imprisoned in the United States. For an analysis of his writings, see Roman Szporluk "Review of *Valentyn Moroz: His Political Ideas in Historical Perspective*, by Valentyn Moroz, Paul L. Gersper, Yaroslav Bihun, and John Kolasky." *Canadian Slavonic Papers / Revue Canadienne Des Slavistes* 18, no. 1 (1976): 80–90. http://www.jstor.org/stable/40867040.
81. Relations between the Soviet Union and China, while never again reaching the boiling point of the Ussuri River crisis of 1969, remained hostile throughout much of the 1980s. Gorbachev's visit to Beijing to meet with Deng Xiaoping shortly before the Tiananmen Square Massacre in June 1989 was an attempt to improve relations between the two countries.
82. Compared to many his predecessors, John Paul II was a very physically fit and active pope. Although he did have surgery on his colon in July 1992 to remove a benign tumor, the rumor of spinal cancer proved to be false.

enced agents, they could eventually use their access to receive, at best, a personal audience with him. Other agents would attempt to gain leadership positions among student groups, and there would be the possibility of acting in other Vatican circles, such as Vatican Radio and the Papal Secretariat.

The Center emphasized the necessity of planning, jointly with the Polish comrades, long-term measures to exercise influence over the pope to in order to reduce international tensions, increase peaceful coexistence and cooperation between governments, influence the political direction of the Vatican in a way favorable to us, and alter its position in regards to various international problems, such as:

- deepen the disagreements between the Vatican and the USA, Israel, and other countries.
- strengthen internal schisms within the Vatican.
- research, develop, and carry out measures to destroy the plans of the Vatican to strengthen monasteries and religious institutions in socialist countries.
- develop KGB contacts in the Russian Orthodox Church, and the Greek and Armenian-Gregorian churches for intelligence work, and to prevent them from establishing contacts with the Vatican.
- open channels through which Polish clergy can revive work in the churches and strengthen their position in the USSR.

In the recent period, party and government contacts in the Polish People's Republic have had a positive evaluation of the Vatican's activities in the international arena and have a positive view of the Vatican's relationship to the Polish government and the Polish Catholic Church. This limited the work that could be done by the MVD in Poland, thus the objective of subdividing this work was done with great caution.

Regarding this connection, in our opinion, there is a danger of damaging the relationship between the Polish government and the Vatican, and the relationship between the Polish government and the Catholic Church in Poland. Because the Church is making so little effort to change things in Poland, it is in our interest to proceed with tact and flexibility to preserve the status quo.

The success of recruiting from the various religious sects depends on the depth of study and proper assessment of the candidate's personal qualities for recruitment, level of intellectual development, behavior, interests, degree of religious faith, relationship with fellow believers in the family, strengths and weaknesses of their character, and the availability of compromising materials. To emphasize again, this kind of work will require a number of religious believers, but not many Poles, because of the fact they will not be able to play a substantial role in a number of the operative tasks. Make sure we prepare for the possibility of using female agents. Their recruitment potential will be evaluated based on whether they are intended to serve as clergy, whether they are working for the illegal press, whether they are replacing elderly clergy, or whether they are leaders of female religious groups. We must be particularly careful about recruiting unbelievers for these positions. Unbelievers should be limited to those who engage in intelligence work.

What follows is an example of a recruitment that strengthened our position. "Zhemaitis" is a Catholic priest in a church in the Baltic. He described his cooperation with the KGB:

> I served in a Church that was often visited by foreign tourists. They were interested in the position of the Church in the USSR, specifically the lack of religious freedom. I had a number of such discussions with tourists, and I was afraid these meetings would cause extreme dissatisfaction among the authorities. In connection with these discussions, my position became very tenuous. I agreed to a proposal of secret assistance from the organs of state security after a brief period of hesitation, because I realized that, if I cooperated, they could defend, advise, and assist me.

To provide another example, KGB agents utilized disagreements between clergy to morally compromise them in each other's eyes. At the first stage of asset recruitment, respect for religious authority in the asset must be compromised through information provided by the KGB from concrete intelligence information of minor risk.[83]

We then calculate that the candidate, when fully engaged by our agents, will begin to provide detailed evidence about religious rivals. Having been informed about his opponents, he not only takes steps to increase his

---

83. Infiltrating institutions, especially religious ones, by finding out about rivalries and then playing off rivals against each other in order to recruit informers, had been a KGB tactic going back to the earliest days of Soviet rule.

dependence on the KGB, but eventually he becomes used to a more positive relationship with our agents. The recruitment meetings, at the decisive stage of this process, already contain in themselves the persuasive fact that the existing cooperation has been necessary, but sometimes the existing dependency must be used as a means of coercion.

One candidate for recruitment, the priest "Valdes," served in one of the most popular churches in Lithuania, which was in a prosperous area. He was a cowardly, weak person. We seized on his financial situation, which was brought about by his small salary. He knew that the local Catholic clergy had criticized him to his fellow religious believers and authorities. Therefore, it was unsurprising that he requested a meeting with the workers in state security organs. Operatives told him that he displayed nationalist feelings, had suspicious contacts with foreigners, and often informed them of his slanted views. "Valdez" replied that these slanderous rumors were motivated by envy, as his contacts with foreigners did not have a secret character, as they took place in the Church and he merely answered questions of the visitors, not displaying nationalist sentiments. Operatives were interested in who may have actually made such nationalist statements, and to whom. "Valdez" said that some priests were noted for engaging in antisocial behavior and were engaged in hostile activities. Operatives recommended that "Valdez" write down his knowledge about which priests engaged in such activities. In the past year, under the pretext of examining new circumstances and verifying certain facts, "Valdez" began to engage in considerable illegal activities. Providing systematic information concerning his rivals, the priest became even more involved with and dependent on the KGB. It was ascertained that he kept his meetings with the Chekists a secret. Intelligence meetings were necessarily kept short. Although he had appeared hesitant, he nonetheless agreed quickly to receive the assistance of our operatives, and agreed to further collaboration with the KGB.

In 1981, the PGU (First Main Directorate) of the KGB drew up new plans to orient the KGB Residents for renewed work in the Vatican.

In Lithuania, with the assistance of the Vatican and Polish groups of priests, several religious extremists created in the Lithuanian SSR a Catholic Committee for the Defense of the Rights of Believers; this was directly connected to events in Poland from 1979 to 1981.

Under the flag of the Church and the nation, this group attempted to unite with other hostile elements to organize anti-Soviet activities and to convert the Catholic Church into open political opposition.[84] This committee printed and distributed illegal anti-Soviet publications, acquired from the West, containing hostile anticommunist information.

The youth in Czechoslovakia do not have a Marxist attitude to the questions of war and peace, international responsibility to the fate of the world, or military service obligations. Our enemies have introduced to them the ideas of pacifism, laboring to use their devotion to abstract-humanistic ideas, by promoting neutralism to negative developments in the socialist sphere and a narrow-minded liberalism. Pacifistic tendencies in the CSSR regarding the activities of dangerous religious sects appear to be dangerous. Peace-making activities of the Catholic churches, which seem to correspond with the general foreign-policy line of the CSSR, may eventually take on a genuinely pacifistic character. Clergy use pacifist slogans in order to win the masses over to their side. Progressive clerical leaders express the hope that the documents of the Worldwide Conference of Religious Statesmen for the Preservation of Humanity from Nuclear Catastrophe, held May 10–14, 1982, will support their views about the place and role of the churches in the fight for peace, by prohibiting the movement of their allies into the fake pacifist side-show.

Chekist organs in the CSSR continue to work on limiting the undesirable activities of Cardinal Tomášek, having expressed to him their displeasure with his subjective, uncritical reactions to the actions of the Vatican, and his unrealistic goals regarding the situation of the Catholic Church in Czechoslovakia.[85]

The security organs are concerned about the existing secret relationship between the bishops in the CSSR, part of the illegal Uniate Church, and

---

84. This is fascinating analysis by the KGB, as it hints that in Poland and Lithuania, the KGB was in battle against the forces of medieval (the Church) and bourgeois (the Nation) nationalism, which merged together in opposition to the Marxism-Leninism of the Soviet regime

85. František Tomášek (1899–1992) was a cardinal and archbishop of Prague, who played a key role in the so-called Velvet Revolution, which saw the end of Communist rule of Czechoslovakia.

their allies in the Intelligentsia. They have conducted religious services in private apartments. The Vatican has in the CSSR two episcopal structures. On questions regarding the so-called illegal Church, the official Church has perhaps not decided yet.

At the assembly of the Chairmen of the Artistic Union and Cultural Institute in Prague on March 11, 1982, Vasiľ Biľak said that Czechoslovakia feels itself under the influence of recent events in Poland, in which the country's communist leadership made political concessions. The Polish workers went on strike, but as of now Czechoslovak workers still engage in minor work on Saturday and Sunday, to provide for themselves.

Due to the events in Poland, the MVD of Czechoslovakia needs to take measures to strengthen operative positions at large industrial enterprises.

Two regiments were created, one in Prague and one in Bratislava, of MVD forces in case of incidents of mass upheaval, and an assessment was made of the opposition in the cities. Out of the 600,000 party members in 1968–1969, 100,000 were expelled.[86] Decisions were made concerning restrictions on the border of the CSSR and Poland, the introduction of new passes for entrance into the CSSR (with the agreement of the existing District Committees of the National Front and the Administration for the Body of National Security in the District), the prohibition of travel into Austria without an Austrian visa, the abolishment of mass travel between the two countries in order to see relatives, restrictions on those living in border regions, including those on the borders with Hungary and the GDR, and restrictions on the activities of religious centers that may be influenced by foreigners in other countries.

Biľak,[87] at the meeting of the Ideological Commission of the Central Committee of the Czechoslovakian Communist Party, on December 10,

---

86. The expulsion refers to the "house-cleaning" of the Czechoslovak Communist Party that occurred during Gustáv Husák's "normalization" from the fall of 1968 to the spring of 1969, when the liberalizing reforms of the Prague Spring were rescinded, and many who had supported them were expelled from the Party. They were viewed by the regime as a potential source of public discontent with the regime.

87. Vasiľ Biľak (1917–2014), was a hard-line communist leader who served as part of the Presidium of the Communist Party of Czechoslovakia.

1981 announced that the party, as an existing entity, much like in Poland, practically does not exist. The international communist movement has developed a negative reputation. Despite the joint efforts of the Czechoslovakian Communist Party with the Communist Party of the Soviet Union to fight world imperialism, the authority of the party has been subverted. He spoke of older tactics of the Communist International, whose decisions were made compulsory for everyone. Now, during every conversation about internationalism, there exist several different ideas about this concept. Jaruzelski used the tactics of maneuvering to a position as leader of the Polish nation and away from his position as a leader of a Marxist-Leninist party. The consolidation of the Polish regime may be completed by 1985, but without assistance, the military regime will not be able to construct socialism.[88]

At the beginning of May 1982, the Central Committee of the Communist Party of Czechoslovakia held a conference of party workers engaged in religious policies. Among those who took part: The Secretary of the Central Committee Foitik, Central Committee Secretary Pezlar, Deputy State Chairman Lugan, Minister of Culture Valak, Head Secretary of Church Affairs for the Government Presidium of CSSR Gruza, workers of state organs of security, and other individuals. The conclusions of the conference:

With the election of John Paul II to the Papal Throne, the Vatican has openly embarked on the path of support of world imperialism and the ideological and political fight between East and West. The task of the Vatican is to divide socialism from the inside. The Vatican has forbidden the Church to engage in movements such as Pacem in Terris, demanded that clerics lead massive religious celebrations connected with the names of Jan Nepomucký, Saint Anezhka, and others, and invited foreign guests to these celebrations.

---

88. Moscow's willingness to allow General Wojciech Jaruzelski to assume leadership of the Polish United Workers' Party in October 1981, on the eve of the crackdown on Solidarity two months later, was a huge concession, evidence of their desperation that there was no one else who could effectively maintain Communist rule in Poland. One of the most important principles of Soviet rule, going back to the days of Lenin, was that military forces had to be strictly subordinate to Party control, in order to prevent the threat of "Bonapartism." Poland's government from 1981 to 1989 was effectively more of a left-wing military junta than a traditional Communist party-state.

The Czechoslovak state is not interested in creating conflicts between the Church and the Vatican, but it will prevent policies that threaten the loyalty of the majority of the population to Socialism. It follows that the task is to prevent the Church in the CSSR from placing the interests of the Vatican before those of the state.

We will determine who is actively pursuing the policies of the Vatican, prevent the growth of these ideas among believers, and deny Pacem in Terris moral, political, and material support. We must exercise our influence to split the Church hierarchy, most of whom, in Prague and the Vatican, are opposed to Pacem in Terris.[89] The conference also criticized some district communist parties, whose attempts at instructing children in Marxism-Leninism have not reduced levels of religious belief.

The meeting called for the carrying out of the aforementioned religious policies in Czechoslovakia to create a path of confrontation between the Vatican and the Czechoslovakian Church. Those called to this challenge are prepared to decisively accomplish it.

The chairman of the KGB in the CSSR, Burdin, in July 1982 stated:

> Cardinals Tomášek and Trnasky and Bishop Gabrish[90] carried out a plan to stop the progressive merger of Czechoslovak Catholic Clergy and Pacem in Terris. Tomášek said that "the pope, as our close neighbor in Krakow, is well acquainted with the situation of the Catholic Church in Czechoslovakia." Bishop Tomášek sent out a letter forbidding all clergy at all levels from joining the organization, concluding his letter with the phrase, "Rome has decided, the Discussion Is Over."

---

89. Taking its name from a reformist encyclical by Pope John XXIII written in 1962, Pacem in Terris ("Peace on Earth") was formed by the Czechoslovakian Communist regime in 1971, ostensibly to promote world peace, but its true purpose was to supervise and manipulate the activities of Catholic clergy in Czechoslovakia. It was one of many religious front organizations formed by the Soviet satellites during the Cold War. The Archbishop of Prague, Frantisek Tomášek, had little control over the organizations' activities, but, as the KGB record states, he forbade Catholic clergy from joining the organization.

90. Julius Gábriš (1913–1987) became Archbishop of Trnava, though his appointment was opposed by the Communist Party.

The progressive mood on the part of the clergy began to diminish, with many walking away from Pacem in Terris. As well, the general secretary of Pacem in Terris, Canon Adler, after twenty-five years of collaboration with state organs and having considered the danger of these associations, desires to leave his position. State organs have attempted to convince the bishop's representative to Moravia, Vicar Bran, and the bishop's representative to the capital, Vicar Gorsky of Brno, to influence Tomášek with letters that were returned without answer.

On June 30, 1982, leading workers of the Party and the state apparatus of Czechoslovakia held a conference to discuss the revision of their policies toward the Church. The main theme of the conference was related to the Roman Catholic Church, and the conference was chaired by the Chairman of the Central Committee Secretariat of the Communist Party of Czechoslovakia, Foitik.

It is self-evident that the state organs of the CSSR have successfully engaged in opposition to the politics of the Vatican. However, Tomášek and Gábriš anticipated that the state organs would undertake certain measures against them and have acted on this belief, and the new position of the Vatican has considerably complicated the situation.

It is necessary to appoint an employee who will work with Cardinal Tomášek, which would involve controlling his activities, as well as monitor his telephone conversations and his written correspondence.

Secretary of the Central Committee of the Communist Party of Slovakia Pezlar noted the strengthening of clerical influence in Slovakia, due to Polish and Hungarian influence, that Hungarian émigrés are comrades with the Church, and this poses a clear threat to socialism. He then announced: "We should not back down, because that would allow liberalism to gain a place here."

The Czechoslovakian Communist leadership expressed worried statements concerning the 1983 visit of the Roman pope to Poland, that the pope's actions have negative consequences for socialist countries, and for the international environment, destabilizing the progress of social normalization in Poland, and would bring about the activization of reactionary Church circles in Czechoslovakia, and consequent acts of resistance to the regime, which the Church will use to exert pressure on the government with the goal of receiving privileges for the Catholic Church in the CSSR.[91]

NOTES

The first Chekist fight against Catholicism was conducted by the baptized atheist Feliks Dzerzhinsky.[92]

On July 1, 1920, Feliks Dzerzhinsky wrote to his deputy I. K. Ksenofontov that the Catholic clergy in Byelorussia and the Ukraine, from the first day of the revolution, demonstrated a hostile mood to Soviet authority, noting:

> In my opinion, clergy have played a large role in espionage and conspiracies. They need to be deactivated. For this, I propose the publishing of a circular to be sent to provinces that all priests must be registered and under supervision. Furthermore, the clergy hear the confessions and fantasies of Catholics, especially women, and this allows them to recruit others for their conspiracies.
> It is necessary to obtain intelligence on these organizations; the key question is which department will manage it.

Two Polish Jokes:

---

91. Unlike Hungary and especially Poland, the Czech regions of Czechoslovakia were among the least religious parts of Europe. Catholics slightly outnumbered Lutherans among its religious inhabitants. In comparison, the areas with a Slovak majority were largely Catholic and much more observant. Slovakia also had an Eastern Rite Catholic community in the eastern regions of the country. As in Western Ukraine, this community was forced underground after the end of the Second World War. This ban against it was lifted in 1968 during the Prague Spring, and was one of the handful of reforms authorized by Alexander Dubček that his successor Gustáv Husák did not rescind following the Warsaw Pact invasion of August 1968. Cardinal František Tomášek was among the most visible opponents of the regime, especially during the period of "normalization" from 1969 to 1989.

92. "Iron" Feliks Dzerzhinsky (1877–1926) was a Polish Communist and Lenin's hand-picked director of the first Soviet secret police force, the Cheka. A ruthless and cruel fanatic, and a capable administrator, Dzerzhinsky established the model for future agents in the symbol of the USSR's security services, the sword and shield.

- At the election of the Roman pope, people were watching for the smoke coming from the building where the Cardinals were meeting. Upon the election of Wojtyła as pope, the smoke changed from black to white, but then suddenly changed to red. Everyone was puzzled, but then someone realized that Wojtyła had just burned his red party card.
- Upon becoming pope, the former Archbishop of Krakow appeared at the Ministry of State Security in Poland and reported, "Comrade Minister, your important government mission has been fulfilled, John Paul II, the Roman pope."[93,94]

---

93. Mitrokhin concludes his transcription with a number of jokes regarding the election of John Paul II, which he may have simply overheard, as opposed to reading in a KGB report. Some Soviet secret police agents were notorious for their mordant sense of humor.

94. The remainder of the document (omitted) lists the names of various people mentioned in Mitrokhin's summary of KGB activities towards the Vatican, including numerous code names, and in some cases real names, of KGB agents who were involved in religious work from the beginnings of Bolshevik rule up to the early 1980s. Some of those identified by Mitrokhin have been revealed by other sources as KGB agents.

Suggestions for Further Reading

Andrew, Christopher and Vasili Mitrokhin. *The Sword and the Shield: The Mitrokhin Archive and the Secret History of the KGB.* New York: Basic Books, 1999.

Andrew, Christopher and Vasili Mitrokhin. *The World was Going Our Way: The KGB and the Battle for the Third World.* New York: Basic Books, 2006.

Andrew, Christopher. *The Mitrokhin Archive II: The KGB in the World.* New York: Penguin Books, 2018.

Ash, Timothy Garton. *The Polish Revolution: Solidarity.* New Haven, CT: Yale University Press, 2002.

Balogh, Margit. *Victim of History: Cardinal Mindszenty, A Biography.* Washington, DC: Catholic University of America Press, 2022.

Cahill, Thomas. *John XXIII: A Life.* New York: Vintage Adult, 2002.

Ebon, Martin. *The Andropov File: The Life and Ideas of Yuri Andropov, the General Secretary of the Communist Party of the USSR.* New York: McGraw-Hill, 1983.

Fejérdy, András. *Pressed by a Double Loyalty: Hungarian Attendance at the Second Vatican Council, 1959–1965.* Matthew Caples, trans. Budapest: Central European University Press, 2016.

Fejérdy, András, ed. *The Vatican "Ostpolitik" 1958–1978: Responsibility and Witness during John XXIII and Paul VI.* Rome: Viella, 2015.

Felak, James Ramon. *The Pope in Poland: The Pilgrimages of John Paul II.* Pittsburgh, PA: University of Pittsburgh Press, 2020.

Gabel, Paul. *And God Created Lenin: Marxism vs. Religion in Russia, 1917–1929.* New York: Prometheus Books, 2005.

Hebblethwaite, Peter. *Paul VI: The First Modern Pope.* New York: Paulist Press, 1993.

Husband, William B. *"Godless Communists": Atheism and Society in Soviet Russia 1917–1932.* Dekalb, IL: Northern Illinois University Press, 2000.

Kengor, Paul. *A Pope and a President: John Paul II, Ronald Reagan, and the Extraordinary Untold Story of the Twentieth Century.* Wilmington, DE: Intercollegiate Studies Institute, 2018.

Kent, Peter C. *The Lonely Cold War of Pius XII: The Roman Catholic Church and the Division of Europe, 1943–1950.* Montreal: McGill-Queen's University Press, 2002.

Koehler, John. *Spies in the Vatican: The Soviet Union's Cold War Against the Catholic Church.* New York: Pegasus Books, 2003.

Kosicki, Piotr H., ed. *Vatican II Behind the Iron Curtain.* Washington, DC: The Catholic University of America Press, 2017.

Mindszenty, József. *Memoirs.* Translated by Richard and Clara Winston. New York: Macmillan, 1974.

Miner, Steven Merritt. *Stalin's Holy War: Religion, Nationalism, and Alliance Politics.* Chapel Hill, NC: The University of North Carolina Press, 2003.

Pelikan, Jaroslav. *Confessor Between East and West: A Portrait of Ukrainian Cardinal Josyf Slipyj.* Grand Rapids, MI: Eerdmans Publishing Company, 1990.

Schattenberg, Susanne. *Brezhnev: The Making of a Statesman.* London: I.B. Tauris, 2021.

Smolkin, Victoria. *A Sacred Space is Never Empty: A History of Soviet Atheism.* Princeton, NJ: Princeton University Press, 2018.

Stehle, Hansjakob. *Eastern Politics of the Vatican, 1917–1979.* Translated by Sandra Smith. Athens, OH: Ohio University Press, 1981.

Taubman, William. *Khrushchev: The Man and His Era.* New York, NY: W.W. Norton and Company, 2004.

Wyszynski, Stefan. *A Freedom Within: The Prison Notes of Stefan Cardinal Wyszynski.* New York, NY: Harcourt Press, 1984.

Index

Andropov, Yuri: appointment as KGB director, 5; second-in-command under Brezhnev, 24, 61; actions against the Greek Catholic Church in Ukraine, 28, 61, actions against the Vatican, 70, 77, 79, 80–81,

Benelli, Cardinal Giovanni: support for *Ostpolitik*, 34; Soviet surveillance of, 64, 82; mentioned by Mitrokhin, 99

Brezhnev, Leonid: comes to power in the USSR, 5, 20; religious belief during era, 18; views towards the Vatican, 22, decline of, 24, 56, 61; hatred in Lithuania for, 27, 56

Casaroli, Archbishop Agostino: support for *Ostpolitik*, 20–21, 26; mentioned by Mitrokhin, 101

Catholics: population size in the Soviet Union, 10–12

De Chardin, Pierre Teilhard: literature targeted by the Soviet regime, 36

Jaruzelski, Wojciech: seizes power in Poland, 24, 94

János Kádár: negotiations with the Vatican, 20–21; 70

Kennedy, President John F.: negotiates release of Slipyj, 19

Khrushchev, Nikita: gives "the Secret Speech" and begins de-Stalinization, 4–5; harassment of religious institutions, 18; release of Archbishop Slipyj, 19, 58; fall from power, 20

Koenig, Cardinal Franz: Soviet surveillance of, 79, 82; support of *Ostpolitik*, 79; mentioned by Mitrokhin, 101

John XXIII: timeline of papacy, 1; support of *Ostpolitik*, 19, 76; election as Pope, 20; views of the Soviet government towards, 25, 75; *Pacem in Terris* encyclical, 19

John Paul II: timeline of papacy, 1; opposition to Communism, 23–24, 87; lack of support for *Ostpolitik*, 23; support for *Solidarnosc*, 24; views of the Soviet government towards, 31, 59, 87–88; election of, 79, 94, 98; mentioned by Mitrokhin, 99–100

Lenin, Vladimir: views towards religion, 8; commemorated in naming of Leningrad, 10; expulsion of opponents from the Soviet Union, 37

Leo XIII: views towards socialism as expressed in *Rerum Novarum*, 9

Lithuanian Catholic Church: KGB actions towards, 14, 25, 52, 57, 83; connection to nationalist protests, 23, 27, 29; freedom of action of, 51

Lelotte, Fernand: literature targeted by the Soviet regime, 36, 40–41

Marx, Karl: views towards religion, 7–8

Mindszenty, Cardinal József: persecution by Hungarian Communist Regime, 18; exile in American embassy in Budapest, 19–20, 70, 76; opposition to *Ostpolitik*, 21–22

Mitrokhin, Vasili: background of, 2–4; gradual emergence as an opponent of the Soviet regime, 4–5; creation of his secret archive and defection to the United Kingdom, 5–6; summary of his archive and its conclusions, 25–26, 31–33; summaries of, 61, 98; errors made by, 69; revelations of "illegals," 72

Molotov, Vyacheslav: meeting with Stanislaus Orlemanski, 13

Organization of Ukrainian Nationalists (OUN): views of the Soviet government towards, 59, 64–65

Orlemanski, Father Stanislaus: visit to Moscow and meeting with Molotov and Stalin, 13–14; punishment by Vatican, 14

Ostpolitik (of the Vatican): definition of, 1, 19, 21; Soviet government's views of, 22; Vatican's abandonment of, 23; Casaroli and, 26; Benelli and, 34

Pacem in Terris (movement): inspiration for, 19, 95; Vatican rejection of, 94; activities in Czechoslovakia, 95–96

Paul VI: timeline of papacy, 1; support of *Ostpolitik*, 19–21, 23, 34, 76; Soviet views of, 25, 29, 53, 81–82; Soviet actions towards, 62, 74, 77–78; position towards Pinochet's regime in Chile, 80

Pius IX: views towards Marxism, 9

Pius XI: views towards Communism as expressed in *Divini Redemptoris*, 10

Pius XII: views towards the Soviet Union, 1, 17–18, 31, 82, 87

Russian Orthodox Church: persecution by the Soviet regime, 11–12, 37, 42; attempted absorption of the Ukrainian Greek Catholic Church, 12, 16–17, 58, 66; sent representatives to the Second Vatican Council, 20, 74; and 1977 "conference," 30; participation in the World Council of Churches, 31, 75; Soviet government's use of, 36, 43, 63, 76, 85, 89

Schaffran, Bishop Gerhard: attempted manipulation by the Stasi, 63; mentioned by Mitrokhin, 105

Second Vatican Council: Soviet attempts to penetrate, 20, 74; Hungarian attempts to penetrate, 21

Sheptytsky, Metropolitan Andrei: attitude towards the Germans, 15; acceptance of Soviet government, 16; death of, 16, 58; views of the Soviet government towards, 64

Sheptytsky, Archdeacon Kliment: Soviet allegations of support for Nazi regime, 66; mentioned by Mitrokhin, 104

Slipyj, Metropolitan Josef: opposition to Soviet regime, 16–18, 58; release from prison, 19; opposition to Vatican *Ostpolitik,* 22; attempts by the Soviet government to discredit his supporters, 28; views of the Soviet government towards, 58; actions by the Soviet government against, 59–60, 75, 78, 83; meeting with John Paul II, 59; mentioned by Mitrokhin, 98, 103

Solidarnosc (Solidarity): origins of, 24

Stalin, Josef: death of, 3–4, 18; change of position towards the Orthodox Church, 12, 43; views towards the Catholic Church, 13–14; persecution of the Ukrainian Greek Catholic Church, 14, 16–17; split from Tito, 77

Starkus, Bishop: quote, v, 23; opposition to the Soviet regime, 27, 50

Synod of Lviv: origins and results, 16–18; legacy, 58

Tomášek, Cardinal František: background of, 92; opposition to Pacem in Terris and the Czechoslovak Communist Regime, 95–97; mentioned by Mitrokhin, 104

Ukrainian Greek Catholic Church (Byzantine Rite Catholic Church, Uniate Church): origins of, 11–12, 33; Soviet persecution of, 15–18, 28–29, 46, 64–69, 76, 83–84, 92; connection to Ukrainian nationalism, 14–15; Soviet belief in Vatican support for, 28, 58–61, 63, 70, 75, 78

Wyszynski, Cardinal Stefan: mentorship of John Paul II, 23, 45; views of the Soviet government towards, 45, 85; KGB efforts against, 67; mentioned by Mitrokhin, 99

www.ingramcontent.com/pod-product-compliance
Lightning Source LLC
Chambersburg PA
CBHW022009120526
44592CB00034B/753